MOUNTAINS, LOCHS & LONELY SPOTS

A TOUR THROUGH SCOTLAND IN A VW CAMPERVAN

STEVE ROACH

Amazon Reviews for Steve Roach's Travel Books

Cycles, Tents and Two Young Gents

Steve's description of the places and people they meet is superb, France is a hard country to crack, and this story shows just how hard it can be. I loved Cycles Tents and Two Young Gents. I have travelled extensively in Europe, on bicycle, motorcycle and camper, and have experienced a lot of the things that Steve and J experienced.
By Simon McCool

I laughed from the first sentence till the last. I have learned more from this book than all of the expert touring books put together.
By mstar12

I laughed out loud more times than I can remember. After several years of not cycling, I am looking forward to a new bike early next year and I am planning on doing some minor touring myself. Its books like this that only make that dream more appealing. My hat's off to the gentlemen who did this tour and wrote about it.
By irishbill76

This is not a serious travel book - but a light hearted tale of a real blokey trip across France. It made me laugh several times. Shades of Three Men in a Boat here. Two unfit young men blundering their way through France. Very amusing and well-written.
By Kew "kbports" (england)

Next Time, We're Flying Somewhere Sunny:

'Packed with anecdotes and tales of adventure that will inspire any would-be traveller.'
Camper & Bus Magazine

This must count as one of the most realistic travel books I've ever read, from picking up the VW to returning to Dover it was so difficult to put down that the phone went unanswered and the dog learnt how to cross her legs. It should be required reading for anyone who is to attempt the containment for the first time, perhaps even handed out at the port of embarkation. A truly Gold Star read. It is so good that it forms my first review with over 80 books on my Kindle.
By Farmer Giles

STEP IT UP!

A very enjoyable book, mainly because I have been to some of the places Steve visited on his travels, it was good to read about places like New Orleans, Florida and the Keys.The places Steve stayed in varied a lot in price and facilities, some were down right awful and unsafe. I laughed out loud a couple of times, its a easy book to pick up and put down without having to remember too much.
By jill in Derby (east mids uk)

I took a punt on this as have only recently been introduced to the world of Kindle and was contemplating a trip to the States. The book follows the author and his better half around the US, with plenty of information on various attractions and a few witty anecdotes from the journey. Recommended for anyone interested in travel and the amusement that ensues.
By Ash

MOUNTAINS, LOCHS &
LONELY SPOTS

MOUNTAINS, LOCHS &
LONELY SPOTS

CONTENTS

Hawick
Abington
Loudoun Castle Theme Park (Abandoned)
Pollock
Gartloch
Dumbarton
Cardross
Cruachan (Power Station)
Oban
Glenfinnan Monument, Loch Shiel
A Bit of History
Mallaig
Skye
Sligachan
Portree
Uig
North Loop to Staffin
Kyle of Lochalsh
Balmacara
Highlands
Urquhart Castle
Loch Ness
Aviemore
Pitlochry
The Wallace Monument (Stirling)
The Dunmore Pineapple
The Falkirk Wheel
Fife Coast Tourist Route
Pettycur
Edinburgh
Berwick-Upon-Tweed
Hawick
Home

MOUNTAINS, LOCHS &
LONELY SPOTS

Hawick – Abington

We pick up the campervan today. We just have to drive up to Hawick, a small town in the Scottish Borders and collect her. I say 'her' because the van is called Sally. In the campervan hire business, I've learned, vehicles aren't just machines – they're almost a part of the family. They have names. They have their own individual characters.

We set off in the pouring rain, the heater on full to clear the misty windscreen. The world is like the inside of a car wash, the M6 a dull grey ribbon of misery cutting through it. The car is lashed by the rain, thrumming on the roof, and we're almost blown into the hard shoulder by a particularly strong gust of wind. Last time we went on a trip like this, I promised Steph that we'd be going somewhere sunny next time. It turns out that I may have inadvertently lied. At least she's not in tears yet. Life hasn't yet beaten her down enough that she can't nurse a small glimmer of hope that the weather might get better.

The scenery either side of the motorway is magnificent, great big hills looming up on either side, their peaks shrouded in cloud. Although most people associate beautiful scenery with glorious sunshine, something that undoubtedly brightens up the landscape and improves the distant views, I've never minded gloom, particularly when it's on an epic scale. It helps that we're relatively warm and dry inside the car – gloomy scenery isn't quite so enjoyable when you're actually standing in it, dripping wet, boots squelching every time you move. But to view it from some sort of comfort can be a marvellous thing, and I enjoy these miles heading up towards Penrith.

Our little dog Clementine has come with us on this adventure, and she's been immaculately well behaved so far, laid out across Steph's lap and dozing contentedly. The key to owning a dog that travels well in vehicles is simple – get them started early. A puppy has a limited period during infancy where it won't be frightened of very much at all. Every day brings new things to explore and everything is exciting. This period is critical for conditioning them for future behaviour, something that most dog owners don't seem to be aware of. We took Clem to puppy training classes and the result is a dog that's generally well behaved at all times. She's used to being in a car, used to being told to sit and so on. She's toilet trained, thank the Lord. She's used to people and, perhaps most importantly, used to mixing with other dogs.

We stop at Tebay Services to give Clem a chance to have a wee and a sniff around the car park. Steph and I share the contents of a flask of coffee. It's already saved us a fortune.

As we carry on past Penrith, heading up to Carlisle, our in-car conversation hits new heights.

'Do you think sheep feel the cold?' asks Steph.

'I guess so. But then they're probably used to it, being outdoors all the time.

With their big, woolly coats on.'

Sometimes, I miss the car stereo (it stopped working about a year ago).

Shortly afterwards, I notice a herd of cows under a tree in a field.

'Look! Cows obviously feel the cold. Or the wet, anyway.'

'Oh, yeah.'

'Do you think they're all intelligent enough to head to that tree for shelter, or do you think there's just one cow that went over and the rest followed him to see what he was doing? Like, half the cows are standing around going 'What the fuck am I doing here?''

Steph makes an observation from the Bible, something about it saying that God gave man the ability to make choices but not animals. She points out that animals make choices all the time, even cows. Little Clem is a very intelligent beastie – whenever she wants to go out, for instance, she sits by the front door and waits for us to take her. Clearly, that is a choice on her part not to do a big dump in the house but to wait and do it outside.

Has Steph just disproved the legitimacy of the Bible, or even the existence of God? It's deep stuff for a wet Monday morning on the M6. Later, though, she ruins any illusion of profound intelligence when we see a sign that says 'Glasgow 96   Edinburgh 93' and asks: 'Is Edinburgh really only 3 miles from Glasgow?'

We leave the M6 at J44 and head north on the A7. Shortly after Longtown we see a 'Welcome to Scotland' sign and cross the border.

The B711 is a single track road that splits off the A7 a couple of miles shy of Hawick. We're heading for a place called Roberton, home of Classic Camper Holidays. Within minutes, we realise that we're really heading out into the sticks, that the road is taking us through some of the wildest, most open scenery we've seen so far. Every now and then are passing places, tiny inlets to pull over and let cars coming the opposite way pass by.

But we don't see any other cars. Things get a bit weird when we find a farmer's gate blocking the road. This isn't a farm track, remember, but a bona fide highway of the national road system. I pull over, get out into the sheeting rain and open the gate. Then I have to drive through and stop again to get out and close it. I could have left it, but after watching Withnail and I too many times as a youth I know the dangers of leaving farmers' gates open. Randy bulls can escape and give helpless locals one int' knee.

Things get even weirder when, a couple of miles later, there's another gate. Just where in the hell are we? I open it, drive through and close it again.

We haven't seen another car for about fifteen minutes. There are no people. We pass by a small lake.

'That's where they dispose of the bodies around here,' I say.

'I was thinking exactly the same thing.'

Thankfully, as we crest a small hill, Classic Camper Holidays swings into view. There's a lovely big wooden chalet nestled next to a brook, and a white T25 van parked on the edge of the driveway. As we get closer, we see a veranda stretching alongside the house and Sally, a bright orange 1972 Westfalia pop-top T2 is parked beneath it.

We park up and Ian comes out to welcome us. He's a wiry feller with a big smile, clutching a roll-up. We shake hands and he bids us welcome.

Shortly after, Becca emerges with their

dog, a wee Jack Russel called Fergus. In moments, Clem and Fergus are jumping all over each other having a whale of a time.

Although the business has been running for a number of years, Ian and Becca only bought it from the original owner back in February, so it's all relatively new to them. They have a fleet of five campervans and will shortly acquire one that's fully kitted out for disabled people, who aren't much accommodated for in the campervan business. It's been a very busy first season, and the vans have been rented more or less without a pause.

Ian gives me a brief rundown of Sally. I remember some of it from last time (with Monty, the hire van for the Europe trip), but the interior is laid out in a different way and it takes me a while to get used to it all. Perhaps the biggest change is that Sally is a left hand drive. This may prove a little harder to adjust to.

Before long, the business side of things is taken care of and I unload the car and put everything into the van. And then it's time to go. They wish us a good trip and we drive off down the narrow road, thankfully not the way we came, although this means continuing along the B711 for almost twice as long as before. The left hand drive immediately proves itself to be a disorienting experience, mainly because we're also on the left hand side of the road. More than once, Steph tells me (in a tight, high pitched voice) to get back onto the correct side. If I stop concentrating, my mind wants to position my body on the normal, default position above the road, which in my car would mean I'm sitting just on the inside of the centre line. In Sally, this means that Steph is well over the line, sitting and staring at potentially oncoming traffic.

It's a slow drive towards Buccleuch as I

get used to the van. I'm extremely grateful that there are still no other cars around as, if I'd gotten into a position where I'd have been forced to reverse, there would have been carnage. Other things are easier than I remember, such as the gears. In our previous campervan, I remember getting into all sorts of trouble on the journey from the hire place to my house, a bitter and anger filled episode involving the M5 motorway, a traffic jam, and a van that wouldn't get into first gear. In Sally, the gears are no problem, as long as they're delicately handled. The only problem would be the lack of ability to change from 2nd to 1st whilst moving, which would mean stopping the van completely at traffic islands in order to start moving again. No big deal and I soon became used to it.

We stop after about half an hour so I can grab a quick cigarette. I park up between two mountains, remove the key from the ignition and get out. Steph follows with Clem, even though it's pissing down and blowing a gale. Smoke over, we all get back in the van and I suddenly find that the ignition key no longer works. I think that Sally might be fitted with some sort of locking mechanism, and fiddle around until I admit defeat. I phone Ian and Becca but they're out, so I leave a message on their answerphone. When I hang up, Steph says:

'Aren't there two keys on that keyring?'

Indeed there are. And the other one fires up the ignition immediately. I can't believe what has just happened. Ah, well.

Our route carries on along the singletrack road for about 20 miles or so, until we find the wider A708 and I can relax a little. It's a mystery why some of these very minor roads, winding their way through some of the most isolated scenery in the country, couldn't have been built 10ft wider. To illustrate this, a look at the map reveals that there are no other roads directly south of Buccleuch for over 15 miles. It's just mountains and hills, valleys and grass and forest. Surely another 10ft width to the road wouldn't make any difference at all?

St Mary's Loch is a beautiful vista, a blue jewel nestled amongst some low hills. The road's empty and we have the place to ourselves. It reminds us of what we expected from Lake Garda in Italy, peace and quiet and stunning scenery. This, with the road running alongside the loch for a short stretch, is far lovelier. No contest. And there's no-one here. There are no little stony beaches, no ice cream vans parked up waiting for business. No screaming children. The weather this far north is obviously a factor in that, as is the time of year.

I remember when I cycled from John O'Groats to Land's End, some 15 years ago, I was disappointed with Scotland in that it wasn't as wild as I'd imagined. I remember moaning about the odd pylon and the way the land had been divided up with fences and stone walls. Pish. Now that I'm older and have seen a bit more of the world, I appreciate these last wild spaces of the UK for what they are, even if there's a house in the view, or a road snaking through the landscape.

This said, we're soon back on a motorway, the M74 heading in the direction of dirty, crowded Glasgow. We get as far as Abington services before pulling off to get some food. Ordinarily, I would never pay motorway services prices for food unless I'm really desperate, but I'm starving. I park up, straddling 2 spaces in the half empty car park. It'll be a while yet before I get the hang of the size of this campervan – they may look small but they certainly feel a whole lot bigger when trying to turn into a narrow space marked with two white lines.

I head inside and check out the Burger King menu, and then head back out to report my findings to Steph. She settles on a veggie bean burger and I plump for a Chicken Royale with cheese. The cost is staggering, but it needs to be done. We sit in the van and eat, and I wonder where the hell we're going to end up sleeping tonight. The original itinerary would have had us up by Loch Lomond somewhere but time just seems to have whizzed by and put the kybosh on that idea. It is still doable, I guess, but I'm knackered and don't really fancy another couple of hours behind the wheel. As we're heading up towards Glasgow, and the industrialised, heavily populated belt between the Clyde and the Forth, I imagine that nice quiet campsites are going to be a bit thin on the ground.

By the time we've eaten and given Clem a little walk, it's about an hour away from getting dark, the early night helped on by the heavily overcast sky. I see a couple of motorhomes parked up and head inside to enquire about overnight parking. For the price of £10 we can join them, should we wish. I think about it for a few seconds, imagining the alternative:

We keep driving, heading into the built up suburbs of Glasgow. It gets dark and we have to keep going in order to clear the city perimeters and try to find a campsite on the other side. We'll eventually find one and I'll be knackered, in no mood to start figuring out how to make the bed and store all of our gear out of the way. I'll get ratty, Steph will tell me to stop moaning, which will make me even more ratty. I know, from bitter experience, that trying to find a campsite in the dark and then messing about in the cold is a nightmare.

We'll argue.

Clem will start barking.

There'll be uproar.

Forget it.

'OK,' I say to the guy. 'Here's a tenner.'

I pay and head back outside to break the good news to Steph, saying that I've enquired about campsites and found a place that has great facilities – clean toilets and even a shop. I tell her we need to get there before dark, so we'll need to get moving. She puts her seatbelt on and Clem settles down in her lap. I belt up and start the engine.

'Are you all set?' I ask.

'Yep.'

'OK then.'

I drive forward and say that I'll need to turn around. I reverse into a space next to one of the other campers. Instead of driving away again, I pull on the handbrake.

'We're here!' I say brightly, expecting Steph to be relieved that we're sorted for tonight. She doesn't look very happy at all.

'Are you joking?'

I explain the benefits of staying here for the first night.

For the sake of decency, I'll censor what Steph said next, but the next time I went to the toilet I had to look in the mirror to check that my ears weren't bleeding.

I try and rearrange our stuff to give

myself room to make the bed. When preparing for this trip, I'd assumed that Sally would have the same layout as our previous van, and that plastic crates would work as an ingenious way of storing all of our gear. I'd allowed two small crates each, for our clothes and toiletries, plus a messenger bag each for stuff we'd want to carry around. There was a further crate for our camping gear, such as a cooker (not necessary) and our plates, cups and cutlery and so on. Then there was the large plastic bag with our double duvet stuffed into it. And the double sleeping bag. Now, trying to move things off the rear shelf to make up the bed, all these crates and bags suddenly seem like a really stupid idea. Everything is in the way, until Steph mentions that the roof is one that pops up and suddenly I have enough extra storage to be able to crack on with the bed. Even so, it's dark by the time I've finished.

Perhaps the most difficult thing is getting the duvet cover on. Usually, I'm a master at this sort of thing. I have the system nailed. Every time I do this at home, I wonder at all those people who still struggle with such an easy task. They key, of course, is to turn the cover inside out, grab the corners of the duvet in the corners of the cover, and shake until the cover falls down, no longer inside out. Once done, it's an easy matter to fasten the buttons at the bottom. However, all of this requires room for shaking and faffing about. Inside a campervan, there is no such room.

Clem has no food. I head into the services and discover that they have no dog food either. Luckily, I have a tin of tuna and this, together with some crumbled biscuits, makes Clem's dinner

for the night. I don't think she minds in the slightest, but we make a note to buy some proper grub for her in the morning.

The reason you are reading about Clem's dinner and other such nonsense is because, at some point, I had to take the trouble to write all of this stuff down somewhere. Had I not, conversations regarding cold sheep and decision making cows would have since been long forgotten, and this book would be very short. For example, today would have read: Got up and had some breakfast. Picked up the campervan. Drove a bit. Saw a loch. Spent the night at a service station. The point about writing down everything that happens, even the stupid bits, is that it gives a full picture of what it's like to embark upon a similar trip, and if that idea wasn't somewhere in the back of your mind then you probably wouldn't be reading this in the first place.

The travel books I like are the ones that don't necessarily detail fun-filled and exciting adventures in exotic places. They're the ones where people in the Arctic are arguing over a biscuit, or where a trip to a posh hotel in Dubai is derailed by a cut foot and a trip to a manky hospital. I used to hate the travel programmes on tv where a wrinkly, bright orange Judith Chalmers has a wonderful time in typical Sunday Times travel destinations. They weren't the kind of travel adventures that interested me. I know that some people reading this will vehemently disagree, but the most interesting travel programmes I've seen in years are the ones with Karl Pilkington, where he pretty much hated most of the places he visited. Chinese pensioners hawking phlegm on a bus, or Mexican lunatics throwing fireworks at each other. Some of the best travel writing books I've read are about visits to places I'd never visit in a million years, and the books merely confirm my convictions. That doesn't mean I hate the books - far from it.

I pull rank as the official trip chronicler and leave Steph and Clem in the van (no dogs are allowed in the services) and head into the warm, well-lit restaurant to scribble all of the day's happenings down whilst sipping at a mug of hot coffee. I feel guilty but it has to be done.

I'm finished by about 9pm, and ready for some sleep. Steph is happily curled up on the bed, writing her own journal. I sit in the front passenger seat and wait for her to finish. Bored, I nip back out to go to the loo and as I'm trudging across the car park I realise that it hasn't stopped raining all day. The last trip was like this, somewhat grim and underwhelming. That got better, and this will too. I mean, it can't go on raining like this for much longer.

Can it?

Loudoun Castle Theme Park (Abandoned)

We don't get much sleep. I wake at 2:30am thinking – hoping – it might be between 6-7am so we can pack up and clear off but no. Some arsehole is parked up close by with his engine running, despite the car park being nearly empty and this being a sleeping zone.

Irritated, I get dressed and head out for a confrontation. It all goes well, in that I don't return to the van with a knife sticking out of my kidney, but the damage has been done. We're all wide awake and Steph needs the toilet.

She emerges already dressed and with Clem on her lead. We walk over to the services and find a sign on the door saying it's closed. Closed?! It re-opens at 3am, which is 10 minutes away. It's too cold to stand around, and we're getting lashed by the rain even though we're under the glass canopy of the services building. The trees in the car park, good 25ft'ers, are shaking violently. By sheer luck, we've parked Sally in the one place – right in front of a solid bank of trees – where the elevated roof won't be torn off.

We can't wait around in these conditions. Small print on the sign says that the nearby petrol station will be open, so we walk over and use their facilities. I buy a couple of coffees from their vending machine and we trudge back to the van and drink them in silence. I daren't ask what Steph is thinking. She'd probably scream and throw the coffee in my face.

We finish the coffees and get back into the still-warm bed. Clem, wet and shivering, forces her way under the duvet. Can't blame her. We manage to get some sleep but even so I'm up at 8am. Whilst Steph gets dressed and takes Clem for a wander around the car park, I take all of the crates down from the roof area and have a bit of a sort out in the van. There is plenty of storage space, here and there, and I whittle down some of our belongings by stowing it away. Hopefully things should be a little easier from now on.

We buy more coffee for breakfast and, after making the bed back into a settee and pulling down the roof, we set off about 9am. It's a stone's throw to the M74, which we leave at J8 and head down the A71 towards Galston. The first place we pass through is Stonehouse.

Scores of boxy, pebbledashed buildings form an estate. We see graffiti, litter, and adolescents in tracksuits sitting on a wall outside some shops, looking at Sally as we drive by.

We stop at a supermarket and I head inside for some dog food. I get £100 from an ATM and am momentarily taken aback when some weird money comes out of it. I'd forgotten they have their own currency in Scotland. As far as I'm aware, it's exactly the same as English money except for the pictures. This said, English money isn't technically legal tender in Scotland, and can be refused, though that would simply be a matter of national pride getting in the way of a financial benefit, something the Scots aren't renowned for.

One of the themes of this book concerns the abandoned wrecks and ruins that man has left behind, in particular some of the larger structures that have been left to decay. During the following pages, we will be visiting an abandoned theme park, a wreck of a mental asylum and even a building topped with an enormous concrete pineapple. I find the idea that people could let such enormous and costly projects slide into ruin fascinating. So do a number of other people, who call themselves 'urban explorers'.

Much of the world we live in is invisible to us. For a start, a staggering amount of building work has been carried out beneath our feet, literally out of sight. There are nuclear bunkers, telecommunications facilities, tube systems, engineering plants, hospitals, sewers, service tunnels, even Channel Tunnels. The general population is aware of these things in just a very basic way, a dim knowledge that such things exist. We never actually see any of this

stuff. Very rarely does anyone ask themself what it would be like to go and explore these places.

Wouldn't it be amazing to stand beneath the streets of London, inside a storm drainage system that's as big as a small cathedral? Or visit one of the tube stations that are currently deactivated, a platform and track and no other people? Walk through the grim corridors of an abandoned lunatic asylum, peering through the tiny slits in cell doors that once housed the poor souls deemed insane? All these places are close by, silently brooding and collapsing whilst society populates the well-maintained areas, virtually oblivious to their existence.

But seeing this world is not easy. Much of the interesting stuff is off-limits to the casual explorer, either blocked off with fences or locked doors, or, in the case of Ministry of Defence property, human and/or canine security guards. Many ruined properties are privately owned, and the last thing the owners want is for people to be trespassing and injuring themselves, so pretty much everywhere is signed with warnings preventing unauthorised access.

You can wander happily around a functioning railway station (such as Euston) whilst the lights are on and shops are trading, but if the same station fell out of use fifty years ago and was now a far more interesting version of itself, with weeds growing through the floor tiles and creeping vines lacing their way up the walls and through the broken windows, then it's likely that you wouldn't be permitted to go anywhere near the place.

Fortunately, for the curious people who would like a closer look at our off-limits heritage, there are websites and even books that tell you how to go about it. For the basics, I would recommend 'Access All Areas' by Ninjalicious, a book you can easily find on Amazon that details etiquette and necessary equipment, and provides information on gaining entry to all manner of areas that would ordinarily be impossible to see.

At Galston (home of the now extinct Galston Hardball game, a primitive version of squash played against the wall of Barr Castle), we turn onto the A719 and it's only a couple of miles to our first destination – Loudoun Castle Theme Park.

From 1995 to 2010, this was a family park with various rollercoasters, mechanical rides and a log flume, all overseen by cartoonish mascot Rory the Lion. Owner Henk Bembom ploughed millions of pounds into improving the park, turning it into one of the country's premier family destinations. A Scottish Disneyworld, if you like.

In 2007, an employee fell from a rollercoaster track when the ride had become stuck and he climbed up to try and push it forward. His subsequent death led to a trial where the owner was eventually cleared of any negligence. The verdict didn't come until 2010, legal wheels turning in their usual, tortuously slow manner, and this period must have weighed heavily on the mind of Bembom when considering the future of the park. This, together with the terrible Scottish weather and the low turnouts during wet and windy days, led to a decision to close the park in 2010. It was no longer a commercially viable prospect. It probably never had been.

Today, the park is abandoned. Many of the rides have been sold off and shipped to various theme parks, but some remain, slowly and silently rusting away.

When researching places to visit during the trip, this quickly rose to the top of the list. As a writer, the chance to visit an almost apocalyptic piece of scenery simply couldn't be passed up. I read as much as I could about the place and even emailed the owner for permission to have a look around.

There is no trespass law in Scotland, so I could have simply arrived and found a way into the site. Of the ruined places I planned to visit, this was the only one where I though such a precaution was the wise option. The email bounced back as undeliverable.

We arrive to find that the local area still has little brown road signs advertising the theme park, and I briefly wonder if my information is out of date. When we pull up at the entrance, however, an even larger sign informs us that the site is most definitely closed and strictly no admittance is allowed. A big set of iron gates blocks the road leading into the park. One of these gates is open.

I park the van and clamber into the back to fetch my camera. Steph feels a little uneasy about entering the site and decides to stay put, even though she badly wants to take a look around. As I'm faffing about, a silver car pulls up and the driver gets out and starts to close the gate.

'Hello!' I cry, lurching from the van to have a word.

He looks at me suspiciously.

'Is this place closed then?' I ask. It couldn't have been more obvious.

'Yes.'

'Do you think I'd be able to come in and have a look around?'

'Not a chance. They're private grounds, closed to the public.'

Damn. He asks me if we've seen a post van come through the gate and I say that we haven't. He thinks about closing the gate and leaves it open. As he turns to walk back to the car, I walk after him. There's no way I'm letting this one go.

'I've driven a very long way to see this place,' I say, putting on my best begging face. 'Wouldn't I just be able to have a quick ten minute look around? I tried emailing Mr Bembom but the email came back as undeliverable.'

With an air of resignation, and a small amount of reluctance, he gets out a mobile phone and makes a call. I hear him as he asks someone at the other end if it's OK. He hangs up. I await his decision with my breath caught in my throat.

'OK,' he says. 'But leave the vehicle where it is and you'll have to walk.'

Relief floods through me.

'No problem. Will it be OK if my girlfriend and little dog come with me?'

'Your girlfriend will be fine, but not the dog. No dogs.'

I can't see what difference having a dog

will make when walking around an empty theme park but I don't press the point. I've been really lucky to get authorisation and I don't want to blow it. I thank him and he gets back into his car and drives away.

'Well?' asks Steph.

I explain the situation. She offers to stay behind and look after Clem. I can tell she's gutted but there's no way either of us would leave little Clem in a vehicle unattended.

I begin the long walk up the avenue. It leads to a gentle crest after a tenth of a mile, and only then can I see the actual public entrance to the park. The road splits, the right hand fork leading off to the car parks and the left fork blocked by three cute little blue and white ticket booths. The paint is still reasonably fresh, not yet battered by the perma-drizzle. As is the colouring on the nearby sign:

Welcome to Loudoun Castle!
What's On?

High Dive Stunt Show	*1pm*
Rory the Lion Show	*2pm*
High Dive Stunt Show	*3pm*

And, at the bottom, a lion with welcoming paws spread wide, a green, three-pronged crown on his head: 'Enjoy your day!'

Past the booths, the road widens out to reveal the ruins of Loudoun Castle itself. Formerly a 16th Century tower house, the building has been extended at least twice and was at its most magnificent in 1941, the year the interior was destroyed by a fire. All that stands now is the outer shell and some of the internal structure. It's a haunting sight, empty and abandoned. The view through the windows at the front reveals open sky and trees growing inside the ruins.

It's fenced off, so any kind of entry is forbidden. One of the few remaining interior wooden window shutters is hanging from a hinge, clapping against the stonework in boisterous applause at my visit. I see the remains of a turret, precariously balanced and stretching the boundaries of physics as it remains standing against seemingly impossible odds. It looks so fragile, as though it could collapse at any moment.

Behind the castle, a short wall-lined driveway leads to a gatehouse. I walk through the open archway and the theme park is laid before me.

The first thing I see is the remains of a rollercoaster, the looping dull orange track barely standing out against the equally dull grey sky. This is the carcass of the Twist N' Shout coaster, and from what I see is the most likely candidate for the unfortunate death of the park employee back in 2007. It's fenced off and the tarmac area in front is beginning to crack and succumb to weeds. Grass is starting to grow in thickets, unchecked.

I take a wander over and try to imagine crowds of people here, the noise as the coaster rattles around the track. Children eating ice cream, parents taking photos. People whooping with enjoyment and fear. It's hard to picture. For some reason, it looks like the rollercoaster has always been this way.

Further into the park, I can see another coaster in the distance, behind which is a huge silvery sphere. I take a walk through the drizzle for a closer look, past

empty areas where rides have been moved off site and nature is slowly reclaiming the space.

The coaster, smaller than the previous one, is the remains of The Rat, one of those rides with sharp corners that make sudden , violent turns. It looks further into the process of decay than the Twist N' Shout, the foliage is higher and the colours more faded. The ride itself looks terrifying, the tallest section of track held up by supports no thicker than an arm. The steps leading down into the waiting area are covered with grass.

I can't imagine It'll be too long before The Rat rusts and buckles, and sections start to collapse.

The big silvery sphere turns out to be an enormous model of the moon. Surrounded by a thick steel collar (painted red), seats hang at ground level, secured by long chains. This is a Chair-O-Planes ride, where the chairs are spun around the outside of the moon, lifting into the air through the force of centrifugal gravity.

This ride, right here, is the largest example of its kind in the world. It squats, forlorn and unused. Decommissioned. Redundant. The red steel is just starting to become frayed and rusty at the corner joints. The great silver globe, pockmarked with little

moon craters, is becoming stained and rusty at the joints where the fabricated steelwork panels meet. Paint is flaking away, revealing the dull gleam of metal beneath. It's a sad sight.

These are the three main attractions I see. The rest of the park contains various huts and shops, surrounded by rotting wooden benches. It's all sodden and damp. All of it falling into ruin as the days pass. A few more seasonal shifts, a few more changes between heat and cold, rain and sun, and the lot will collapse.

Nothing is permanent. Once mankind has gone, a few million years will see everything we've built turn to dust. It's terrifying the speed at which it happens. Two years ago, these rides were still in use!

In all this time, I've had the park to myself. There are a few cars parked up, signs that people are on site but I see none of them. There's an administration building and a couple of Portakabins. I pull up my hood and take a few final pictures, which the incessant drizzle will ruin by spotting the lens. As I'm halfway back to the toll booths, the silver car reappears and the man gets out.

'Well?' he asks.

'It's amazing,' I say. 'I know that it's a terrible thing for the owner, but to see something like this, the way it is now…. Listen, can you thank him for me? I really appreciate the opportunity.'

'No problem, son.'

'Has he any plans to reopen the place as a theme park?'

'Not with this weather. Nobody comes.'

'It's rained ever since we got to Scotland,' I say.

'It hasn't stopped raining for the last five years. Cheery-bye.'

He gets back in his car and drives off again, leaving me to walk back through the gatehouse and past the castle alone. I notice a house off to the right, lights on and lived in. I wonder if the owner is in there, watching me wander around his abandoned dream.

Pollock – Gartloch – (Glasgow)

It's a long walk back to the van but I'm happy. I'm glad I got to see the theme park with some sort of authorisation and didn't have to try to sneak in. Because I would have tried and it would probably have ended in carnage, being eaten by guard dogs or something equally as grisly.

We carry on along the A719 through the village of Moscow (supposedly named after Russian refugees of the Crimean war who lived in the area for a while). There are just over a hundred people living here. The local area north of the village is known as 'Little Russia'.

We rejoin the M77 motorway and the GPS flashes a low battery warning. Our next destination is Gartcosh, a small village to the north-east of Glasgow. A quick look at the map reveals an indecipherable concentration of major and minor roads, and no easy way of following it on the fly. The cigarette lighter is, believe it or not, built into the back of the driver's seat and the GPS lead won't stretch between that and the windscreen. We could try and navigate using the road atlas or pull over for a coffee and give the GPS a quick charge. It's an easy decision.

We exit the motorway at J2 and head for Pollock's Silverburn shopping centre to grab a coffee. I volunteer to fetch the drinks and Steph stays in the van to look after Clem.

The mall is huge, a self-contained universe of capitalist extravaganzas. I'm shocked at the size of it, and stand in dumbstruck silence for a few moments.

I ask a shopper if they know where the toilets are and follow their directions. It's quite a walk, and I get the impression I've hardly seen anything – further cathedral sized corridors lead deeper into the centre, all bright lights and enormous window displays of stuff I can't afford to buy. On the way back from the khasi, I notice a Starbucks and head in to buy a latte and a mocha. I might need to remortgage a house to be able to afford their extortionate prices but at least some of the cost is being funnelled back into the UK economic system via Corporate Tax. I mean, I can sleep soundly at night safe in the knowledge that one of the most aggressive American companies to invade our country and kill off the indigenous competition is at least putting a few million pounds back into the system. That's one less thing to get angry about, right?

My feet are aching by the time I get back to the van, a combination of the miles clocked up already this morning and a choice of ill fitting, flat-soled trainers.

Coffee drunk and GPS charged, we head back onto the M77, switch to the M80 and the M8, a route that takes us through central Glasgow. It's bigger than I expected, and from the motorway we can see a mix of modern and old architecture. In the distance, we see a few enormous blocks of flats. Some of the nearer buildings are even bigger - boxy and featureless with thousands of window apertures. What on earth goes on inside those buildings?

We're soon out on the other side of the city, passing through suburbia. All big cities are surrounded by a ring of inner-city suburbia, much like a ring of scum around an old plughole. These areas are often rough-holes full of poverty, crime and violence. This looks no different.

A couple of miles further out we enter the Gartcosh area, and zone in on the next fun-filled attraction on our itinerary – the Gartloch Hospital (aka the Gartloch Mental Asylum), now abandoned.

The hospital, an imposing Victorian gothic building straight out of a horror movie, was commissioned by the City of Glasgow City Lunacy Board (I kid you not) in the late 19th Century. Opened in 1896, it had a capacity of just over 540 beds. Within a decade, capacity had risen to 830. One can only imagine what it must have been like inside the hospital when it was fully operational and chock full of mental patients. Up to 50 of these beds were used for victims of tuberculosis, and overall numbers dropped back down to former levels by 1909.

During World War 2, the hospital shipped out all of its psychiatric patients to other hospitals and focussed on becoming an emergency medical centre, helping to ease the national crisis of young men coming back from Europe with bits blown off them.

Outside the grounds in front of the hospital is a commemorative stone monument laid into the grass, dated 1977 and created to mark the occasion of the Queen's Jubilee. It is still brightly coloured and features a picture of the hospital with what appears to be a double-scooped chocolate ice cream in front of it. Whatever the decision making process was behind this, I have no idea, but wonder if perhaps one of the inmates was asked to come up with something.

Exactly a hundred years after it opened, the hospital closed for business and has stood empty ever since. Time hasn't been kind during the years leading to our visit. Although the outer shell of the main building remains in superb shape, the interior has been exposed to the elements and is little more than a ruin. During my research phase, I noted that pictures on the internet showed empty ground floor window apertures, and climbing inside the building looked like it would be a doddle. However, upon our arrival, we see that the ground floor windows are now boarded up and a 6ft perimeter fence surrounds not only the hospital but also the many smaller outbuildings. Signs warn about the consequences of unauthorised entry.

With it being broad daylight, and with the rather pertinent obstacles of the fence and window boards, I decide not to try and force my way inside. There's a development office nearby, so I head there asking for permission but it's closed. Instead, I make do with a

wander around the perimeter and take a few photos.

The building itself is huge, another example of the grand scale which the Victorian builders and engineers embraced so enthusiastically. It's essentially three storeys high, with an extra storey for the central column and a further 2 storeys on top for the towers on either side. It's a cliché, but even without the history of what the building was used for, it retains a brooding presence. Even in daylight, the glassless windows on the upper floors are dark and thoroughly uninviting. Around the back, signs of decay are more pronounced, the courtyard buried under a thick carpet of wild grass and weeds.

The outbuildings are also showing signs of extreme fatigue. Render is falling away, brickwork is stained with damp. Grass runs riot in the courtyards but, surprisingly, the creepers are only just beginning to find purchase.

It's a short, lonely tour.

The site is now earmarked for redevelopment. A huge billboard advertises 'Gartloch Village', a proposed estate where dwellers can experience the joy of country living just a few miles from the bustle of Glasgow. The pictures all look wonderful. The downloadable PDF brochure makes no mention of the hospital's historical function as a mental asylum, and most of the 12 pages in the brochure feature images of nature (brightly coloured flowers, shafts of sunlight split by trees, dandelion seeds and so on), and very little about what the village itself will look and feel like. The few houses pictured are all brown boxes with no interesting architectural features. Are they really going to pull down these fascinating Victorian beauties and replace them with brown brick boxes? One promising sign is that the asylum is rendered inside the brochure in watercolour, and it appears that the main building will remain, externally at least, structurally intact as the interiors are converted into flats. Confirmation is difficult as the information on the development website is as scant as it is in the brochure. It all feels like a pipe dream, a corporate idea that's gotten as far as the marketing stage but no further.

The hospital and surrounding area are pretty grim. It's going to take a lot of work to make things as pretty as they are in the brochure, and one suspects that they are still negotiating financing. Part of me hopes they don't achieve it, particularly if they do plan to raze down all of the various outbuildings. The other part of me is glad that the main building, at least, will be reused. Living in a flat here would be amazing. Provided, of course, you don't mind the ghostly wailings of former patients, as per the multiple EVP (Electronic Voice Phenomenon) recordings posted on YouTube.

It's been a very odd day so far, with this and the abandoned theme park at one end of the spectrum and the mall at Pollock right at the other, one an illustration of mankind's current peaking of civilisation and the others examples of what happens when it all goes wrong and everybody leaves. All three sites are connected in a fundamental way – by money, a dark current that underpins virtually every aspect of life. Places like Loudoun Castle Theme Park and the asylum at Gartloch don't just fall into ruin for no good reason – they do so because the money runs out.

I rejoin Steph, out giving Clem a walk on the orderly grassland in front of the hospital. We all get back in the van and I drive away, enjoying one last look at the asylum building. Ten minutes later, we're heading back through the city of Glasgow and then out onto the other side, this time driving across a spectacular bridge that straddles the river Clyde.

Dumbarton - Cardross

At Dumbarton, we stop at a small trading estate and I head inside the Homebase store in search of a bucket. Steph has been griping about the lack of toilet facilities in the van, and I have so far neglected my promise to secure a bucket for any piddling emergencies. Despite the romanticism of being on the road and adrift of society, her attitude towards squatting and pissing in a layby hasn't softened.

I find the aisle with buckets and spend a couple of minutes pondering the options. Like anything these days, buying any required item isn't as easy as it once was. There's far too much choice. If there had only been one type of bucket, I'd have paid and been out of the store by now, but with three different types I'm forced to weigh up the pros and cons. The cheapest bucket is black and rather flimsy. If Steph's had a good drink, she might sit down on it during a drunken, 3am widdle and it might collapse beneath her, resulting in an arse full of bucket shrapnel and a van full of piss. The most expensive bucket costs about 14 pounds, and whilst it's a fine example of Man's proficiency in bucket making, that's far too much money to waste. This said, it is the most sturdy of all three buckets on offer, and being the only yellow one it offers an aesthetically pleasing choice if not a fiscal one, which essentially complicates things still further. In the end, I take the easiest route and buy the mid-priced bucket, which seems sturdy enough and cheap enough to make both of us happy. Purchase complete, I return it to the van and tell Steph that we now have en-suite facilities.

She looks at me with a disappointed expression.

'Couldn't you have got a bigger one?' she asks.

'It holds three gallons! How big is your bladder?'

A nearby M&S lures me inside, primarily because we need some easy-to-prepare meals for the times we decide to do our own cooking. Our own single-hob camping cooker remains unused, as Ian and Becca kindly provided a two-hob cooker with the van. Although Steph's a great cook (in that she manages to make a variety of vegetarian meals tasty enough for my carnivorous self to manage without meat for short stretches), there simply isn't the room or equipment within the van to create anything from scratch. If the weather was more clement, and we had the patience, I daresay we'd have discovered this wasn't the case, but for now I decide to go with a few tins that we can quickly heat the contents to produce a half-decent meal.

Although I find M&S food to be slightly over-rated, they do a delicious range of tinned curries, of which the hot beef curry is their finest. It is, in my opinion, better than many curries served in authentic Indian restaurants. I grab a couple, and an armful of expensive vegetarian tinned soups. Thus provisioned, I feel comfortable in the knowledge that we can head off into the

true wilderness of Scotland and hopefully survive.

It's a short drive to Cardross, home of the third abandoned site we plan on visiting. For any readers growing concerned that this is turning out to be a book about empty buildings, fear not – it just so happens that 3 of the 4 ruins we plan to visit during the trip are all within close proximity to each other and it makes sense to see them all on the same day. Although I could happily spend a week drifting around looking at such things, Steph is already tiring of the urban exploration experience, and is itchy to get some more touristy visits under her belt.

Cardross is a large village, with direct rail links to both Edinburgh and Glasgow. Robert the Bruce died here, though the manor house he once lived in has long since disappeared and only a field remains.

St Peter's Seminary, the reason we are here, is a building that has fallen into an advanced state of ruin, a staggering accomplishment seeing as it was only completed in 1966.

A huge structure made primarily of concrete, the architecture is brutalist in style (named after the French term béton brut, for 'raw concrete') and is such that it has been called 'a building of world significance' by one of the international architecture conservation organisations. In 1992 it was granted category 'A' status protection. Prospect magazine named the seminary as 'Scotland's greatest post World War 2 building'. All of this means little in the tangible world, and the building continues to decay as the days go by.

Designed to house 100 students of the Roman Catholic faith, for whatever reason the site never quite achieved full capacity. Within 14 years of opening, the budding monks has all gone and the use of the building was recategorised as a drug rehabilitation centre. Less than a decade later, by the late 1980's, the site was vacated and immediately started falling into ruin.

Situated a good half mile north-east of the village, the building is reached by a muddy track leading alongside a golf course and through a small wood. It really isn't the kind of place that anybody would pass by accident. Such a remote and awkward location contributed heavily towards its decline, particularly with regards to keeping water from entering the building. Although concrete is pretty much insoluble, the maintenance issues proved even more so. Today, much of the internal structure has collapsed and only the outer shell remains intact.

The GPS leads us to the start of a track that leads to the site, but it turns out to be barred by an 8ft metal fence. Part of this has been kicked down so a small gap remains which can be climbed through. Steph and Clem stay in the van whilst I check it out. I walk so far and check my progress against the GPS on my phone. It looks like it might be a 20 minute walk each way. I inspect the satellite view and see that if we go through the village and attempt a different track, there might be a quicker route.

Ten minutes later, we're parked up at the edge of a housing estate, looking at a well-used farm track that looks far too bumpy and potholed to take a campervan up. We get out and start walking. The track curves around to the right, past somebody's house, and reaches a fork. To the left, the track deteriorates into a muddy path. To the right, another set of 8ft iron fencing bars the way. Except that this time, the fence literally only covers the track and can be walked around on either side. We carry on and the trees open up to give us a view of the golf course. As it's still raining, the course is empty. Minutes later, we're back amongst the trees, and the track – now also a muddy footpath – splinters off in various directions. Tracking the site on my phone GPS, we attempt to reach it by trial and error, eventually finding our way to yet another high metal fence, behind which looms the seminary.

From this angle, it literally looks like a multi-storey car park. Levels layered one above the other, covered in dark pebbledash and graffiti. It's like something from the set of The Warriors.

'I don't like it,' says Steph, peering into the surrounding woods with an anxious expression. 'It looks like a crack den.'

She's not wrong. One of the bits of graffiti warns 'KEEP OUT!'

I examine the fence. The gated section is chained and padlocked, the top of the fence covered with ugly spikes. Nobody has forced their way in before us from what we can see. The fence leads deeper into the woods, marking the perimeter of the site.

'I'm going to take a look and see if there's a way in.'

'Hurry up.'

'Aren't you coming with me?'

'I just want to go.'

I leave her with Clem and follow the fence. As expected, it's not too long before I find a way in. I walk up a set of damp stone steps and find myself in a concrete corridor littered with debris. I can't see the view I was expecting from my internet research, the main central area surrounded by concrete balustrades. I venture a little further inside and am stopped in my tracks by a bang from one of the small side corridors, and the sound of something shuffling. It doesn't sound like an animal. I wait, listening. Another shuffling sound is followed by silence.

Someone else is here already. I wonder whether or not to carry on. I think of the 'KEEP OUT' graffiti, and the remoteness – this would be an excellent site for a shooting gallery, and I have no way of knowing how many people might be on site. With various bits of tech kit on me, I'm a muggable prospect, and though a couple of junkies wouldn't bother me it might be different if I'd inadvertently bumbled into some sort of skag haunt or local gang hangout. Damn. If I was alone, I'd probably chance it, but I can't help but think about Steph and Clem being out front and in full view. If this place is in use, anybody could come along and see them.

I decide that it's for the best if we leave. It's a hard decision, because I can almost feel the pull of the building, beckoning me deeper inside, but a lack of preparation on my part has left the three of us in a place I know very little about and even a small risk of us not being safe here should over-ride any selfish reasons for staying to take more photos. We've seen a couple of great places already today, so writing off the seminary isn't that great a loss.

Quietly, I head back outside and go back to Steph. She looks relieved to see me.

'Did you get in?' she asks.

'Yeah, but I think someone else is in there. Let's go.'

We find our way back easily enough, but by the time we reach the van Clem is filthy from all the puddles she's walked through.

It's a short drive to the southern edge of Loch Lomond, and we follow the road along the western side. The loch is obscured from view by a continuous guard rail and a solid line of trees. We get the occasional glimpse but it's gone before we can enjoy it.

It'll be dark soon. I'm knackered and don't fancy the drive to Oban. Maybe we should find somewhere to camp around here.

We continue driving until we happen upon 'Loch Lomond Holiday Park' and pull in for the night. We get a pitch and hook up to the electric. Cameras and the electric toothbrush are put on to charge. I make the bed and climb in for a kip.

Steph wakes me at 8pm and shows me around the site. It's very nice, and our pitch overlooks the loch, which is a dark, inky presence reflecting slivers of moonlight. There's a games room, complete with a huge tv, dvd player and a pool table. We could happily spend the rest of the evening in here but unfortunately they don't allow dogs. I suppose we could have put Clem in the van on her own for a few hours but neither of us wants to do that. She's one of us. If she can't go in, we won't go in.

Despite the new purchases from M&S, we simply boil the kettle and eat a Pot Noodle each. After that, we take a wander down to the shore and look across the dark waters of the loch before settling in for an early night.

Cruachan (Power Station) – Oban – Glenfinnan Monument, Loch Shiel

I wake at half seven and extricate myself from the bed without waking

Steph. I grab my camera and wander down to the shore of Loch Lomond to take a few pictures. The morning is crisp and the sun is no more than a glow behind one of the mountains. The water is perfectly calm and flat. It's all very lovely and peaceful. I head across to the floating jetty and walk along its length, suspended above the deepening water by a thin metal grille that lets me peer into the depths below. As I stand there taking photos of the scenery, the sun appears. A very gentle tide gives the jetty an almost imperceptible motion.

Back at the van, I wake Steph and she takes Clem for a walk. I then begin the long process of getting ready to leave, something which will be familiar to people who own a campervan.

I pack any stuff we've had out overnight away into the plastic crates, and change into some clean clothes. The rest of the crates are cleared from the roof area and dumped outside, and then the roof is pulled down and secured. It would be incomprehensible to head off anywhere without first drinking a cup of coffee, so I set up the stove and boil the kettle. Once done, the electric cable is unhooked and tidily coiled. I check the oil, an absolute must for a van this old – an engine seizure would kill it. Once the coffees are drunk, I reconfigure the bed into a settee (after first rolling up the sleeping bag and duvet and tying them with a bungee), pack away the crates and other paraphernalia into the storage spaces and get rid of the rubbish. By this point, the cooker has cooled down, so I stow that back into position. Finally, we take turns with our ablutions in the nearby toilet block and we're ready to go.

In all, it's a process that takes 90 minutes or so. It's a chore that I mostly carry out alone, as two people would just get in each other's way. Plus, my marginal obsessive compulsive tendencies mean that I have to make sure everything is done correctly. Some readers may think that all of the above could somehow be condensed, the list of things to be done made shorter. Certain things could be left undone. Whilst the set of tasks could be examined for a reduction in time and labour, I should point out that doing so would result in a total collapse of order.

We set off alongside the northern end of Loch Lomond on a ribbon of road hugging the shore, before turning off onto the A85 towards Oban. Shortly after, we're driving alongside Loch Awe when Steph shouts out 'Powerstation!' This doesn't mean she has a desperate need to hear a cd featuring the late Robert Palmer and the boys from Duran Duran, but that we're passing a place she'd found a tourist leaflet for, something she considered would be interesting for a boring arsehole with an interest in unconventional places, such as myself. That's not to say that in the absence of anything better to do she wouldn't tag along and take a look. After all, who in their right mind would pass up the opportunity to see an electricity generation station that had been constructed inside the hollowed out core of a mountain?

As you might guess, no dogs are allowed, and Steph is resigned to the fact that once again she'll be sitting in the van dog-sitting whilst I go off gallivanting. I could have left it. We could have carried on. But that would simply deprive you, dear reader, of witnessing (second hand) the unbelievable feat of engineering we are about to encounter together. So, whilst Steph sits in the van and mulls over what a shit holiday she's having yet again, I say 'Blame the readers!' and scootle off.

I'm disappointed to learn that no cameras are allowed, and ask if they might make an exception for a writer currently working on a book about Scotland. My plea is rebuffed, although they do give me a brochure and tell me to contact the marketing department if I have any questions. Five minutes later, I'm sitting on a shuttle bus at the back of the visitor centre, and the tour gets underway.

Our guide is a bespectacled man called Dougie, and he gives a brief introduction talk. The site is owned and operated by Scottish Power. On the nearby mountain of Ben Cruachan, a man-made dam blockades up to ten million cubic metres of water in a natural basin. When the dam was completed, it apparently took just ten months for the basin to fill to capacity. I put my hand up and interrupt him to check this fact, and he confirms it.

That's how much it rains in Scotland.

The site operates only during times of peak demand – first thing in the morning, when everyone's showering and boiling kettles in preparation for going to work, and at teatime and the part of the evening when the adverts marking the break in Coronation Street prompt a rush for the kettle by millions. With no electrical storage on site, all generated electricity is sent straight onto the National Grid.

The electricity is generated by running water from the dammed reservoir through a number of steep pipes through the mountain. The water hits the turbines and creates the necessary spin. It is then channelled through a surge chamber to slow it down, and finally released back into Loch Awe. One would think that such a high volume of liquid would have disastrous consequences for the Loch, but it's so big that even if all of the water were emptied into it, levels in the loch would rise by just one inch.

At night, the turbines are reversed using electricity bought back from the National Grid (the tariff is cheaper at night), and water is pumped from the loch back up the mountain to refill the reservoir.

Dougie explains all of this in a humourous and well practiced manner. He asks if we're ready to see the outage site for all that water and when we all agree he instructs driver Ian to begin the tour. Ian turns on the ignition, drives five yards and parks up again.

'We're here,' announces Dougie, deadpan.

It's a brilliant start to a thoroughly engaging tour. To our right, a small, fenced-off pond shows signs of movement, with the odd tiny vortex appearing on the surface. Dougie points out that just one turbine is running at the moment. Should all four be in operation, the surface of the pond would be bubbling like a jaccuzi.

When Ian starts the engine again, the tour begins in earnest, and we're shortly at a tunnel entrance marking the start of our descent into the heart of the mountain. At a kilometre long, and gently sloping downwards, the tunnel makes us really feel like we're being taken somewhere special, and it's hard not to imagine the millions of tonnes of rock pressing down above our heads.

It took six years to build the power station, a process that involved dynamiting a way into the mountain and excavating 220,000 cubic metres of rock and spoil, some of which was used in the construction of the visitor centre. It was opened in 1965 by Queen Elizabeth II.

When the bus parks up at the end of the tunnel, we step outside into a surprising level of humidity. A few doors lead to places we'll never see, but one takes us up a flight of stone steps towards the viewing gallery. A display of materials used to construct the power station is laid out on a ledge, interspersed by large pots with sub-tropical plants growing out of them. Despite the complete lack of natural sunlight, the plants survive with minimal tending, thriving in the heat and sucking moisture out of the air. To our sides, the corridor walls are damp, a result of surface water (some 400m above us) trickling through the porous mountain rock. An experiment some years previously tested how long this process took by adding blue dye to the water and seeing how much time elapsed before it appeared in the tunnels. It took just two years to filter through.

We're led up to the viewing gallery and shown a series of wall-mounted pictures of the excavations. Nobody is really interested, of course, we all just want to see what's behind the screen blocking the large plate glass windows. When Dougie presses a button to raise the screen, the main chamber comes into view.

We're at roof height, looking down, and the first things we see are the four enormous yellow turbines, laid out in a row and receding towards the back of the chamber. Between them, they can generate 440MW of electricity. They look like toys, the bright yellow playthings of giants.

Gradually, my gaze leaves the turbines to take in the chamber itself. At 90 metres long and some 36 metres in height, it's big enough to accommodate not only a standard football pitch but a seven storey building plonked on top of it. It's huge. And all of this is inside a mountain that, from the outside, looks just like any other. You could walk or drive right past it without suspecting for a moment that the inside has been hollowed out and filled with gigantic bits of machinery.

The viewing gallery is a small room, and with almost twenty people inside it we're forced to rotate positions to get a decent view of the chamber. When everyone is satisfied, Dougie begins talking once more, and, amazingly, everyone gravitates towards him and leaves space for me to go back to the window and take in a more leisurely view. This, to me, is just as beautiful as a loch in sunshine, and I'm stunned that the others have come all this way and are satisfied with a look that lasts no more than a couple of minutes. Personally, I'd have loved to get into the chamber and walk around at floor level, with these yellow monsters towering over me, thrumming with power as their unseen workings spin at 500-600 rpm. Alas, it's not to be, and before we know it we're walking back down the steps and are shepherded back onto the bus.

Dougie does a headcount, miscounts and tries again. Satisfied that nobody has sloped off, he gives Ian the nod and we're driven back up the tunnel and into bright daylight. In all, the tour takes just over 30 minutes.

I head back to the van and gush about the experience to Steph, who asks me to look after Clem so she can at least have a wander around the gift shop. I oblige, and move the van around the car park so I can get a photo of it in front of the visitor centre. Dougie comes outside and I corral him into the shot.

I'll include a section from the Scottish Power promotional brochure here:

The Legend of Cruachan

The Cailleach Bheur or Bera, (the Old Hag of the Ridges) was the guardian of a fountain that welled up from the peak of Ben Cruachan. It was her duty to cover the spring with a slab of stone at sundown and lift away the rock at sunrise.

One evening she fell asleep and the well overflowed. The water, rushing down the mountainside, burst open a new outlet to the sea through the Pass of Brander. By the time the Cailleach awoke, the water had flooded the wide strath below and drowned all the people and their cattle.

So was formed the River Awe and Loch Awe.

The Cailleach was turned to stone and sits to this day high on the mountain above the Pass of Brander.

When we leave, we drive along a short stretch of road hugging the loch, elevated on concrete stilts. It sounds more exciting than it actually is, as the unusual construction can only be seen when you're not actually on the road.

The scenery really opens up en route to

TERRA FIRMA TRAVELS

Oban, with mountains, forest to our left and Loch Etive to our right. We pull over to fill up at a petrol station, and I'm horrified to learn that half a tank comes in at almost fifty pounds. I'd forgotten just how much juice these campervans can guzzle.

Oban is a pretty town that is slowly succumbing to a side-effect of the Capitalist disease – homogeny. The original port is backed up with the usual sprawl of shops, although there does remain a promising variety of local stores. One day, no doubt, all of this will be Macdonalds and Starbucks, WH Smiths and Spar, but for the moment there is enough of a selection of non-superbranded stores to preserve some sort of identity.

We leave Sally in a car park and walk to the harbour. We see a number of fishing boats, well-used and worn with flaking paint and spots of rust, banked up against the harbour wall. Monstrous seagulls eye us with suspicion, as though we might be hiding food from them. Turning back to face the town, our gaze is drawn up towards McCaig's Tower, a granite folly in a circular shape that resembles a mini Coliseum. The owner and architect John McCaig died before his vision of a museum and art gallery could be built inside the circle, which is no great loss as the area is now a local

park with fantastic views of Kerrera, Lismore and Mull.

One of the things on Steph's ticklist for this trip was to eat some fresh scallops. Readers familiar with my previous travel books will know that she's a vegetarian, but one that eats scallops and prawns. She won't touch any other type of fish, which is just ludicrous, I know. You wouldn't believe the arguments we get into over a can of tuna.

A portable food stall on the harbour front, MacGillivray's Seafood Bar, appears to serve fresh pan fried scallops in hot garlic butter with home made cheesy coleslaw and a crusty baguette. All of this for a tenner. Not being a big fan of scallops myself, I decline, and we sit at one of the wooden benches and wait. A stooped, elderly gent sits down at the next table, sighs, and starts a lengthy display of hawking phlegm and sniffing loudly in an effort to stop stringy bits of snot escaping from his nostrils. Steph looks at me as though she could vomit at any moment and moves to the furthest table.

Her meal, which sounds delightful, appears served in a dull yellow polystyrene tray, the kind found in chip shops, and this takes the shine off the presentation somewhat. Nevertheless, she tucks in and is soon cooing with pleasure. I eat some of the bread, and try some scallop, which just tastes mushy and bland. I am, of course, not a scallop connoseiur. There are 5 of the buggers in the tray, and each has a bright orange appendage that neither of us has seen before. Usually this thing, whatever it is, has been trimmed from the scallop. So far, Steph has left these bits to one side.

I get up and ask another couple eating scallops if the orange bits are safe to eat. They laugh, and point to a pile of orange leftovers on their own trays. They also have no idea what they are. I ask the girl in the stall who cooked them. It takes a little while for her to understand what I'm saying, as she's an Eastern European lass without a brilliant grasp of English, but she eventually laughs and tells me that the orange bits are 'the best bit!' Steph picks at them, unsure.

Later, we enjoy a couple of hot drinks at Coffee Corner, a nice little place with metal tables and chairs outside. Clem sits at Steph's feet and takes a keen interest in people passing by. Although she's a very friendly dog, and always ready to roll over in submission to a complete stranger in order to receive a good tummy tickle, she does have a tendency to turn savage for no particularly obvious reason. Some people she just doesn't seem to like. It could be a young boy eating an ice cream, a man wearing a hat, or an elderly nun enjoying a pleasant stroll in her robes and wimple. So far, we've found no common denominator. Being a terrier, she has something of a hunter-killer buried deep in her psyche, and it does seem to pop up at the most inopportune moments. Thankfully, today she just sits there and doesn't summon enough energy to do anything more than yawn and look cute.

Our waitress brings out the drinks to our table. Being the second person that's served us today, it's funny how she is also Eastern European. Now there's already a lot of debate about 'bloody foreigners' coming into the UK and taking over our jobs, so I won't add to it, but I will say they're generally polite and willing to work hard. And they've come a lot further to take the opportunity than, say, the tracksuit wearing loafers of Stonehouse.

On the way to the Glenfinnan Monument at Loch Shiel, we drive along roads offering some of the most spectacular scenery yet. One of the most important, and often underappreciated things about a touring holiday isn't so much the places one visits when the vehicle stops, but the views that present themselves along the way. It's an obvious thing to state, but if you're going on a grand tour of anywhere, you really do have to love driving. Thankfully, I do, and the part of these huge trips I enjoy the most are the actual travelling bits – I find the journey often turns out to be more memorable than the destination.

One of the things we see whilst driving is so glorious that I stop the van, put on the hazard lights, and get out to gawk and take a few pictures. The few passing motorists don't appreciate my stopping on a hill without a layby, and give their horns an angry blast of disapproval. If they had any sense, they'd have pulled over as well, because they were passing one of the finest sights Britain has to offer.

Castle Stalker squats on a tiny island in Loch Laich, a grey, four storey tower house on a patch of green, surrounded by blue water, with a backdrop of mountains. It really is staggeringly beautiful. Originally a small fort, the structure was added to in the fifteenth century, and fully restored in the twentieth. Now in private ownership, the castle has a history of being passed between various Highland Clans, mostly through murder but once as the result of a drunken bet. What a night that must have been.

Fans of Monty Python may already be familiar with the sight, as it features in the 'Holy Grail' film as The Castle Of Aaaaarrrrrrgggghhh.

We continue towards Glenfinnan, and I tell Steph how amazing it will be, something I know because I've been there before. We arrive, park up and pay the inevitable charge. Only then do I realise that if I'd waited seven minutes we could have parked for free. For once, I don't mind paying, as I consider it a donation to the National Trust, who manage the site.

We cross the road and walk down towards the monument, which is situated at the northern end of Loch Shiel. The setting equals that of Castle Stalker for sheer beauty. The monument, a great stone cylinder, rears up above us, and behind it the loch fades into the distance, edged by mountains that form a 'V' shape and lead your eyes back down to the water. No wonder this image appears in pretty much every Scottish calendar and tourist brochure. And here we are, with the place to ourselves!

Erected in 1815, the monument marks the place where Bonnie Prince Charlie gathered supporters for the 1745 Jacobite Rising, one of a number of ultimately doomed attempts to restore the Stuarts to the thrones of Scotland and England.

Steph takes a wander inside the monument whilst I wait with Clem. A tightly wound spiral stone staircase leads her to the top, where she climbs out and stands next to the stone figure of the 'Unknown Highlander', a symbolic representation of the men who supported the Jacobite cause. She takes a few photos and I wander down to the shore with Clem. The late afternoon light is quite spooky, and I potter about with a camera trying to capture it.

When I'm done, I turn to find Steph exiting the walled area surrounding the monument, and a guy in a hi-vis yellow jacket closes the gate behind her. Where did he come from? Even though Steph isn't afraid of heights, she remarks that her legs have turned to jelly and it was an unnerving experience. I don't much like heights either, but want to head up top to get more pictures. The chap now blocking the gate tells me that I'll need to pay £3.50. I ask him why, as I've already paid £2 just for the pleasure of parking the van. He gruffly states that this is the cost and it's clear that I'm not getting in without paying it.

It's a funny thing being asked for money by a member of an organisation that wasn't even around at the time the very thing he's charging me for was built. They just seemed to have turned up, taken over and started charging. Now, I know the National Trust is much loved and does an exceptional job, on the whole. And I don't mind giving a donation through a parking charge, that's a legitimate and sensible way of charging for the pleasure of visiting the monument, something they 'look after' for the heritage of the country. But

£3.50 to climb some stone steps to take a picture and come back down again? Even if I really milked it, the tour of Glenfinnan Monument would take about 2 minutes. It literally is nothing more than a spiral staircase surrounded by a wall.

I wouldn't even mind paying the parking charge and an extra £4 for a couple of overpriced coffees. The thing that really galls me is the fact that the money being requested isn't really for visiting the monument anyway. After all, it's stood there quite happily for two centuries, enduring the worst weather imaginable with nary a scratch. No, the money is necessary to pay for the brand new modern building that is the coffee shop and gift shop, an extravagance built solely to earn them even more money. There's no need for a gift shop. It's an addition to the site that necessitates a charge for adding it in the first place. No doubt there is an employee tucked away in the back, piddling about with a spreadsheet, and his wages will also need paying. The fellow who seems to exist solely to tell people they need to pay money will also need paying, and surely this is a set of affairs that would cancel each other out in any other world that doesn't have a fascination with 'business models' and twisting every facet of modern life into a money generating enterprise.

Gaah! Enough moaning. We leave.

A Bit of History

Ten thousand years ago, Scotland was empty. Nobody lived there. I can state this with some certainty because there was a sheet of thick ice covering the country, which gradually retreated as the last Ice Age was superseded by a more temperate climate. This gave way to sustained natural growth, and forests soon dominated much of the inland areas, broken up by tracts of marshland and mountains. Animals came, notably bears, boars and wolves.

About seven thousand years ago, the first humans arrived, converging from Scandinavia, Ireland, and England (itself a thoroughfare for humans coming up from Europe). These people were the distant ancestors of the Scots today – all foreigners, coming into a wilderness. These early people lived mainly on the coast and the small islands dotted in the North Sea and the Atlantic Ocean (the Orkneys, Jura, Islay etc.).

In the early Neolithic period (4000BC onwards for Scotland), the people became more settled, planting crops and slowly segueing into a farming based lifestyle. They created better earthenware implements and began building shelters from wood, and occasionally (in places such as Skara Brae) from stone. They placed great importance on their burial sites, and it seems less so on their own houses, putting more effort into looking out for the dead rather than the living.

It's worth noting here that these early people came from areas which had already started developing their own societies, particularly in Europe, and the direction – the influx – is an important feature of the future development of Scotland (or rather the delay of progress). In the same manner that early settlers didn't originate from Scotland, future ideas and cultural advances would also originate from

elsewhere, often creating a lag in development (hence the late arrival of the Neolithic period and subsequent 'Ages'). Ideas would generally come into the country and, for much of its early history, Scotland culturally gave the rest of the world very little.

The Scottish Bronze Age began sometime around 2000BC, when the secrets of metalwork made their way up from Europe. This, of course, led to better weapons and sets a marker for the following millenniums, where much of Scotland's history is wrapped up with violence and warfare. Smaller groups of people began coalescing into larger tribes, due to improvements in farming techniques and the fact that there was an obvious safety in numbers. Around this time, the various tribes began to get a better understanding of each other.

Up until 1200BC, or thereabouts, the Celtic influences and culture that seem so embedded in the history of Scotland (and Ireland) were completely absent. The people that the Romans and the Greeks knew as the 'Celts' originated in southern Europe, and slowly made their way up as far as Scotland by 1200BC. It

seems that they didn't need to invade the country with force – their ironworking techniques and essentially more 'modern' outlook was accepted and embraced by sections of the indigenous population, and the cultures merged without violence, resulting in a dominance of the Celtic culture over time. The Celts would bring with them a caste system, whereby the ruling elite would tend to only breed amongst themselves, a system that would dominate into modern times.

Around 1000BC, hill forts started to appear, a sign that various settlements felt the need for better protection against hostile tribes. The next two and a half thousand years can, on a very simple level, be summarised as having different groups of people fighting each

other, and various outside invaders, as the various nobles and Kings fought to create a unified country.

The first serious threat to the country as a whole came from the Romans, who by the time of Christ had control over most of Europe. Of course, at this point, it's unlikely that anybody in Scotland had the faintest idea who Christ was, as indeed would be the case for much of the rest of the world.

The Romans conquered much of England and made their way north, and their Emperor Agricola decided that he might as well take the rest of Britain as well. By this time, 79AD, the inhabitants of Scotland were thoroughly immersed in an Iron Age culture and they knew how to fight. Agricola called these people the 'Caledonians' (they would later also be known as 'Picts') and it would be five years of fort building and fighting using a scorched-earth policy until the Caledonians were finally defeated. For whatever reason, Agricola didn't immediately capitalise on this success, and the Caledonians regrouped and reclaimed the land.

Emperor Hadrian thought better of heading north to fight and instead built a great wall with the aim of keeping the Caledonians out of England. Subsequent Emperors built and maintained a second wall further north, the Antonine Wall, stretching between the Forth and the Clyde, and for a while the area between the two walls was a military zone. However, the fierce northern tribes beat the Romans back to Hadrian's Wall in 180AD and for a long time that marked the frontier of the Empire. Subsequent Roman invasions in 208AD and 305AD failed to hold territory north of the wall.

Whilst this was a clear win for the Scottish people, in hindsight it proved to be a Pyrrhic victory, effectively stopping dead an influx of more modern Roman ideas and infrastructure improvements. For this reason, Scotland remained in the Iron Age for longer than was necessary.

The 4th Century was a time of much to-ing and fro-ing, as the various tribes repeatedly overran the wall, even getting as far south as London (then 'Londinium') before getting chased back by various Roman generals and their armies. Despite this, there were signs of burgeoning trade between many tribes and the Romans, who, amongst other things, took a particular fancy to Hebridean wool.

The time is also marked by various tribes having their own chiefs and/or kings, which were invariably fighting with each other (a pattern that would continue for well over a thousand years). And, inevitably, right at the end of the century came the first encroachments of Christianity.

During the Scottish Bronze Age, things were happening in the Middle East that would come to shape the world as we know it today. These events, real or symbolic, are summarised in the Bible, a book which acts as a springboard for most of today's major religions. The arrival of the obscure and unknown ideology of a man that died thousands of miles away, hundreds of years earlier, would eventually have a huge impact on Scotland (as, indeed, it would have an impact everywhere else).

With the collapse of the Roman Empire, various tribes would head south to plunder what was left behind. As the tribes in Europe grew in stature, they too would come to Britain to see what they could find. For the next few centuries, the whole of Britain would be subject to repeated invasions, from the Germanic Angles, to the eventual arrival of the fearsome Norsemen from Scandinavia. Many a Saturday afternoon was ruined by the arrival of a bunch of big beardy bastards in a boat, come for a bit of pillage and rape.

Scotland was now primarily composed of Picts, Scots (Gaelic speaking invaders from Ireland), Britons and various other tribes, and they continued to fight amongst themselves and also against the influx of foreigners determined to destroy them.

It would be pointless to go into any kind of detailed history right here, and there are other books that have authors with the necessary patience to engage in such a task. Needless to say, it's a time of great confusion, with various Kings and their heirs murdering and battling each other, and much killing or being killed by successive waves of invaders. In the 250 year period leading to the general hovering of William the Conqueror in Scottish affairs, Scotland would see a blizzard of successive Kings, beginning with one bearing the name Cínaed mac Ailpín, which we know in an Anglicised form as Kenneth McAlpin, an unlikely Royal name if ever there was one. King Ken, if you like. There follows: Domnall (Donald), Causantín (Constantine), Aed, Domnall II, Causantín II, Máel Coluim (Malcolm), Indulf, Dubh, Culein, Cínaed II (Kenneth II), Causantín III, Cínaed III, Grig, Máel Coluim II, Duncan I, Macbeth, Lulach, Máel Coluim III, Domnall III, Duncan II, Domnall III (again), Edgar, Alexander I..... and on it goes. One can see, just by looking at the names, how the kingdom was never safe to one particular tribe, and how foreign invaders often turned up and took over.

As if the power struggles between the rival kings and tribes didn't provide enough turmoil, an increasingly powerful church empire was also flexing its muscles, and it seemed that abbeys and churches were springing up everywhere. With great influence coming from the direction of Rome, various kings formed an allegiance with the church and elevated religion to some considerable power, which it began using to gorge on wealth. In time, the wealth amassed by religion would far exceed that of royalty. Quite why God needs so much money I don't know, but it is a pattern that continues to this day.

If Scottish history is convoluted already, the arrival of the French in Britain complicated matters to the point of incredulity. The English elites traded land with our continental neighbours, as did the Scots, and even the Scots and the English ceded each other various tracts. During the upcoming wars that would engage all three countries to one degree or another, land would be swapped, granted, gifted or forcibly taken away. The countries would form allegiances and break them seemingly on a whim, and betrayal was just another facet of daily life in the power struggles of nations.

It would be easy to summarise Scottish history until 1290 as a succession of squabbling kings determined to take the crown and fighting to keep it. Literally, it is just a long list of names with no corresponding list of developments in art, literature, invention, or episodes of history that would have any real consequence.

Now, thanks to Mel Gibson, the next part of Scottish history becomes a little more well known. Although Braveheart is a very good film, it's no secret that facts have been altered to suit the mechanics of storytelling. Perhaps the best single example I can think of is the relationship between William Wallace and the French Princess Isabella, a relationship summarised in a brutal and hilarious way by Stewart Lee during his 2005 show 'Standup Comedian', filmed in front of a Glasgow audience. (I won't ruin the joke by repeating it here. You can get the dvd on Amazon for less than the cost of a pint of lager, a bargain price that not only let's you see the savage deconstruction of a Scottish national hero but also provides the best opening sequence of any comedic performance yet filmed.)

Author John O'Farrell states that Braveheart couldn't be any more historically inaccurate if 'a plasticine dog had been inserted in the film and the title changed to William Wallace and Gromit.' Whatever the inaccuracies, the resultant increase in tourists as a result of the film boosted Scotland's income by up to £15 million.

There's no doubt that Wallace existed and was indeed a national hero. After the death of Alexander III in 1286 (apparently he fell off his horse whilst drunk), the only legitimate heir to the throne was a young granddaughter known as the 'Maid of Norway', who died in 1290 during the journey to take the kingdom. With no heir, a power struggle between the nobles ensued and thirteen of them squabbled between themselves to 'rightfully' claim the throne. The two with the best chances of proving they were legitimate were Robert Bruce (not the famous Robert The Bruce, that was his son) and John Balliol. Asked to arbitrate proceedings,

and agreeing to do so with a list of concessions set out for any future ruler, English King Edward I chose Balliol, but only after ransacking every vault in England to check if there was some clause that meant he could legitimately claim the throne for himself.

Edward I, aka 'Longshanks' (so called simply because he was tall), used the concessions to undermine and control Balliol as a way of subjugating the kingdom – if he couldn't own it outright, he would endeavour to control it by proxy. Fed up with this state of affairs, Balliol sought allegiance with the French and tried to use this new power to keep Longshanks at bay. Four years after Balliol was crowned, Edward invaded Scotland and deposed him, taking him back to England as a prisoner, thus leading to the state of affairs covered in the Braveheart film.

If you haven't seen the film, I'll summarise the bare bones of what happens next: Wallace appears, as if from nowhere, and plays a key role in defeating the English at the Battle of Stirling in 1297. For this, he was knighted and became the Guardian of Scotland. A year later, however, Wallace and his army were defeated at Falkirk. Wallace escaped, and until his capture and execution in 1305 he remained a major problem, instigating small scale guerrilla campaigns against the English with much success.

As hinted at in the film, which ends with the death of Wallace, attention now switches to Robert The Bruce, son of the aforementioned noble Robert Bruce. Although regarded as a national hero for what was to follow, he was actually a man who had no compunction about switching his allegiances back and forth, depending upon the prize. He had fought for the English against the Scots and had sworn fealty to Edward numerous times.

After the Battle of Falkirk, Bruce accepted the now vacant post of Guardian along with a second man, John Comyn. Comyn was a staunch supporter of the deposed Balliol, and Bruce, sensing the kingship was attainable, was naturally his enemy. In 1306, when Comyn wouldn't pledge his support for Bruce's planned seizure of the throne, Bruce and a few of his supporters murdered him in cold blood at Greyfriars Kirk, a place more famous in modern times for the saga of a devoted dog called 'Greyfriars Bobby', more of which later.

Bruce now had the choice of taking the crown by force or leaving the realm as a fugitive. He chose the former, and immediately set out on a short campaign which included the seizure of Dumfries castle from the English, advertising to the population of Scotland that he could do what Balliol couldn't – make Scotland an independent realm, free from the control of the English.

In Glasgow, a bishop absolved Bruce of his sins, effectively wiping the slate clean in the church's eyes. At the time, there was an order in place that religious officials in Scotland must be Englishmen appointed by Edward, and despite the risk of excommunication by the Pope (a backer of Edward), the church involved itself in the political carnage. The bishop, of course, was Scottish.

Bruce was crowned king in March, but three months later he was a fugitive, his Queen and family members imprisoned in cages, many of his supporters executed for treason. Defeated at the Battle of Methven by an English army,

battered once more at Tyndrum, Bruce narrowly escaped capture and spent the next four months hiding on Rathlin, an island off the coast of northern Ireland.

He spent the next 8 years indulging in guerrilla warfare and strengthening his support base. He used the time to convince the general population that despite his well known trait of switching sides, this time he was committed to Scotland. By 1314, Bruce's army had swelled considerably, and it was enough to decisively beat the English at the Battle of Bannockburn. At a stroke, Scotland was now an independent kingdom.

Robert the Bruce, onetime murderer and fugitive, became a national hero.

Mallaig – Skye - Sligachan

All afternoon, the roads have been leading us into evermore rugged and scenic landscape, and so it continues. Craggy mountains lie all around us. The road undulates as it makes its way seemingly towards the end of the world, the distant landscape containing the remote isles of Rum and Eigg and nothing beyond except thousands of miles of North Atlantic Ocean until the coast of Newfoundland.

I stop on the crest of a large hill to take a couple of photos of a small white building perched on a heathered crag. To my left, a dirt road leads down to a small loch, and a hand painted sign says 'Nae Cars Doon The Track Please'. All around, the clouds press down, grey and leaden.

I'd checked the ferry crossing times and we were in no rush, but I thought we should get the tickets before heading off for a quick tour of Mallaig. I remember, from a trip with a previous girlfriend in what seems almost like another age, we found a small beach at Mallaig, a crescent of golden sand with crystal clear waters lapping at the shore. We'd also taken a dog, and enough camping equipment for a week, and it hardly seems possible that it had all fitted into a Ford Fiesta. At the time, the dog was prohibited from entering the sea by a fiercely territorial swan, which had claimed this little spot of paradise for itself. I wanted to see that little beach again.

Down at the harbour, I park up and enter the ferry administration building, and am surprised to learn that the last ferry leaves in five minutes. They need to update their website! I buy the tickets and head back to the van, relieved that I had the foresight to get the tickets before anything else. I'm disappointed about not having the time to look around Mallaig, but the excitement of going on a ferry eclipses it.

We roll forward and park at the end of the queue. Apart from us, there are only about six or seven other vehicles. At £31.50 for a one way crossing, it's a little pleasure most visitors now forsake in order to take the much quicker (and free) route across the Skye Bridge. We'll be heading back across the bridge, further north at the Kyle of Lochalsh, but I wouldn't have missed the ferry ride for anything. Strange, really, as some of the worst childhood memories I have are of the ferry crossing from Weymouth to Jersey, where my brother and I were dragged at virtual gunpoint by our father into an ordeal that would last for six hours but felt like six months. I was, without fail, always sick on the crossing. My brother did exact some sort of revenge by throwing up over the side

one time – the wind caught it and threw it all over our old man, coating him in a blanket of child-sick. I believe that was the last time we made that journey.

Half an hour is not enough time to get seasick, and it's barely enough time to explore the ferry and enjoy the experience. Steph, who worried at Oban that any particularly large gulls might have tried to grab Clem and carry her off to sea, wisely stays inside with her – it seems far more likely that a strong gust of wind might yet accomplish the unthinkable. And it is very windy indeed once we're out to sea. Lord knows how many hats have been blown away over the years. I rush around taking short video clips and photos of the receding mainland, and climb up onto the top deck to stagger about in the gale for a few more. I have just enough time to wander through the inside of the ferry to get a coffee, and become the bearer of bad news when I eventually inform Steph that there isn't any beer.

A crew member walks over and grabs a few biscuits from a little tub specifically for any four legged passengers, and Clem shows her appreciation by wagging her tail furiously and jumping into his lap.

All too soon we're told to make our way back to our vehicles and we head down into the hold. Before we can get into the van an elderly couple comes over to remark on how lovely Clem is. The woman, who may have learning difficulties or may just be a complete oddball, has a stuffed Garfield cat tucked into the front of her coat. They talk about the Skye Bridge, and are convinced that there's a charge to use it. Like the few other people on this ferry, we'll see them over and over as we make our way around the island.

We drive onto the Armadale shore at the southern end of the island. It's now half-six and will soon be dark. I check the GPS for any campsites and find none, so I check my phone instead and find something. It's near Portree, 38 miles away. Surely, I think, there must be more than this – isn't Skye the kind of place that loves campervans and motorhomes? Surely there must be dozens of sites run by enterprising types who have latched onto the market and can accommodate us? It seems not.

'At least there'll be beautiful scenery everywhere we look until we get to the campsite,' I tell Steph.

Wrong again. Despite my memories of Skye being perhaps the most scenic place I've ever visited – every new corner reveals a picture-postcard view! – it turns out that my memory is not as reliable as I'd thought, at least regarding this part of the island. Although there are some beautiful vistas, the southern part seems to be made of scraggy, Bodmin Moor type landscape, with the odd white house scattered here and there. All well and good – I like Bodmin Moor – but I was hoping for something a bit more vertical.

Knowing that the population of Scotland is relatively small, and mostly concentrated around the cities, it had crossed my mind that if we couldn't find a campsite, we'd be fine parking up in a layby for the night. This part of the country is so remote that it should be considered virtually empty. So it's something of a surprise to find a good number of laybys are already occupied by Gypsies. These aren't Romany Gypsies, with their little wooden caravans and horses cropping the grass verges. These are ones with white caravans and 4x4 Range Rovers parked

in the fields. And it looks like they aren't going anywhere for a while – they have satellite dishes hooked up, and washing lines. For all intents and purposes, it looks like they've been here for a while and aren't moving on anytime soon.

We're forced to keep on driving as darkness falls, and I get pissed off with the complete lack of places to park up for the night. I consider pulling into one of the hotels and asking if we can pay a nominal fee to stay in the car park, but continue driving in the mad hope that we'll see a proper campsite. We pass through Broadford, Dunen and Sconser, and as we pass Loch Sligachan and head up into the mountains, I resign myself to the fact that we'll have to go all the way to Portree and try and find the one campsite we know definitely exists.

And then, as we head over the crest, we see it – caravan lights in the distance, a group of vans and RV's in a field on the right hand side of the road. There are no signs and no mention of it on the GPS, but it's a campsite. We pull in and park up outside the admin office. It's closed but a handwritten sign tells new arrivals to set up anywhere they like and someone will eventually come around and take payment. We don't need telling twice. I pull over into a gravelled area with five or six RV's in it and park. In moments, we're hooked up to the electric and turn on the lights.

And the heater – it's freezing. This hasn't deterred some hardy types from staying in tents. I overhear their conversation as I'm waiting outside the toilet block for Steph. They're talking about climbing mountains. I've never understood the reason why apparently sane people spend days ascending mountains, dealing with huge physical discomfort, extreme weather and, of course, the chance of dying. More people die on mountains than you'd think. Sometimes, on places like Everest, conditions are so tough that dead people are simply left where they are. Right now, there are frozen corpses on Everest that will remain there for the indefinite future. These are people whose friends make the decision to either carry on and reach the summit or abandon the expedition and try to get their friends off the mountain. Astonishingly, many people opt for the summit. They argue that this is a once-in-a-lifetime opportunity, that the huge costs and time involved in organising an expedition means that it may never arise again. Well, you can't let a little thing like someone dying get in the way of that, can you? They're a determined bunch, mountaineers.

I cook up some soup for each of us, and we eat it with a large hunk of dry bread. It might not sound like much, but it's lovely. Pretty much anything you eat on a holiday like this is lovely, and if it's hot food that's even better. We snaffle it down and save a few slops to pour over Clem's dinner.

Later, I go outside for a look at the stars. There aren't any. Low cloud obscures everything, which is a shame because being this remote would surely reward us with a starry display that we'd rarely be honoured with elsewhere. Being this far north, and with it being a year of peaking solar activity, I'd vainly hoped that we might even see some Northern Lights. It's not that unreasonable a thing to expect, but with this cloud there's not even the remotest chance of seeing anything tonight.

Behind us, one of the mountains has a symmetrical, triangular quality to it. It rears up, an inky black pyramid against the purplish night sky. I stand there staring at it whilst I smoke a cigarette. Tomorrow, we'll be exploring much of the island. I hope it doesn't rain.

Portree – Uig – North Loop to Staffin

The next morning, the inside of the van is freezing. It's hard to leave the warm bubble of bed but I want a relatively early start and force myself to get up. With the bed taking up the back half of the van, there's very little room to fiddle about and get dressed, and at times like this it's easy to understand why normal people travel somewhere hot and sunny for a holiday. By the time I'm dressed, in enough layers to make me look like some kind of Michelin Man, I'm bursting for the toilet and have to run to the block. It's a wee that sees me letting out a huge 'Aaah!' sigh of relief that I made it to the urinals in time.

I wash my hands and there's a man at the end of the row of sinks brushing his teeth.

'Morning!' I say, but he doesn't answer.

Back at the van, Steph is up and about. This makes things awkward. I wanted to let her sleep in whilst I quietly brewed up a coffee and caught up on writing my trip journal. Now that she's up, it means that Clem will need walking and I'll have to get stuck into the odious process of reconfiguring the van for the day setup, and it'll probably be another half an hour before I finally get to drink my coffee.

I suddenly remember that I'll be submitting an article about the trip to a magazine and grab my camera to take some pics of the van with the roof still up. I take a few shots with the pyramid mountain in the background. The ever-present cloud and miserable grey colour of the sky doesn't make much of a view, but I try to do what I can with what's on offer. It's funny how real scale is lost unless you have a really expensive camera (or that might just be down to my ineptitude). In reality, the mountain is a hulking presence that looms over the campsite, dominating it. In my photos, it looks like a small hill behind the van.

I crack on with the setup whilst Steph takes Clem off for a walk and returns to do last night's washing up. Soon after, the kettle's on the stove and I'm brewing coffee. It starts to rain. The cloud levels drop and the surrounding mountains become obscured.

Our enjoyment of Skye is mainly going to be down to looking at all the gorgeous scenery, and if it's all going to be blotted out by a grisly curtain of cloud then it's going to be something of an unrewarding day. The only thing we can do is drive around the island and hope for the best.

I check the oil, unhook the electric and inspect the sink to see how we go about filling up the water tank. There's an RV ahead of us, so I turn the van around, park up and wait. When he's done, he pulls away, and before I can get into position, some arsehole in another RV scoots in and parks up in front of the taps. He isn't even staying here – he's come straight in off the main road simply to fill his tanks. I'm fuming but say nothing. A few years ago – even a year ago, to be honest – I'd have stormed out of the van and confronted him. This would no doubt have resulted in an argument, and the campsite would have echoed with some very colourful language. It may even have escalated into a punch up, which I would of course

have won because I was in the right. As it is, I can't be bothered, and we sit and wait for the bugger to finish filling up. It takes forever. Eventually, he gets back in the van and drives off, giving us a little wave of thanks for waiting. Cheeky git. Remarkably, my manners are such that I find myself waving back.

In the pouring rain, I open the side door and bring the hose into the van, shoving the end down the hole next to the sink, and clamber back inside. Steph gets the unenviable duty of standing outside and controlling the tap.

We finally get moving, heading off in the direction of Portree. The signs all show a secondary spelling of Port Righ, which is either a translation of 'King's Port' after a visit by James V, or a bastardisation of Port Ruigheadh, Gaelic for 'slope harbour'. We park up in the central square, and I'm grateful to find that the parking charges are, for once, reasonable at £1.50 for 3 hours.

Portree, despite being the largest town on the island, is really very small. It can be thoroughly explored in about an hour. This said, it's a place where you really have to slow down to appreciate it fully. We start by ordering a couple of big breakfasts at Café Arriba, having been lured in by the sign advertising 'The best cup of coffee on Skye'. That's a lot to live up to, and I warn the waitress that we'll be giving marks out of ten. She finds this more amusing than she ought to, and seems determined to make the coffee live up to expectations.

It's dog friendly, which is rare these days for a place serving food, and most welcome. The waitress gives Clem a little fuss, and we settle ourselves into a window seat overlooking the street below. It feels really cosy, testament to the friendliness of the staff and the interior décor. Steph plumps for a falafel/salad/hummus concoction, which turns out to be an assortment of brightly coloured bits and bobs, and I order a full English. It comes with what is indeed a very nice cup of coffee, and a Stella Artois for Steph.

My food comes with a sausage in the shape of a square, which I believe is called a 'patty' and isn't actually made from a square pig. It's accompanied by the usual beans, mushrooms, fried egg, toast and, of course, bacon. There's also a piece of black pudding, which is about as grisly a thing you could possibly eat first thing in the morning. Whoever thought congealed blood was a tasty way to begin the day was clearly insane.

Quite how a bunch of ingredients such as this came together to become a traditional breakfast is unclear, but its probable origins lie in rural areas as a way of giving manual workers a hearty meal that would see them through the morning. In today's health conscious climate, where far less people are out labouring in fields, a meal with core constituents of bacon and eggs is frowned upon by a lot of people (usually those promoting a diet of some sort), but during the 1920's there was a publicity campaign promoting such a meal as a hearty dish recommended by physicians. There's an interesting story behind this, so I'll digress a little. Edward Bernays, nephew of Sigmund Freud, was a member of the Committee of Public Information during World War 1, and his propaganda in getting the general public to support the war effort led him to wonder if the same techniques would work during subsequent peacetime. One of the things he chose to promote – for

financial reward, it goes without saying - was bacon. He conducted a survey of doctors, essentially getting them to agree to the reasonable assumption that a hearty breakfast was a good way for everyone to begin their day. He then sent a primitive form of a mailshot to 5000 doctors, explaining that the results of the survey should be disseminated to the public as a health recommendation. As an example of a hearty breakfast, Bernays earned his money from the bacon producers by thoroughly recommending bacon as the perfect way to start the day. Thus one of the earliest commercial promotional campaigns was born, and very successful it was too.

As a further aside, a typical English breakfast up until the 17th century consisted of ale, bread and beef.

Clem sits quietly, nibbling at bits of black pudding and trimmed bacon. Steph tells me to stop messing about and give her the rind as well, but I don't cave in. Clem's a very fussy eater, it has to be said, and she turns her nose up at the dog food we give her, even the expensive stuff with little beef fillets in gravy. These dinners often look better than some of the crap I eat. We're not going to solve the issue by giving her human food, despite the adoring gazes she uses on us to share what we have.

As we're eating, an old gent takes a tumble and everyone looks over to see if he's alright. He stands, brushes himself down and hobbles out. There's a step in the café that's about four inches or so in height, and if it wasn't for the fact that it's painted in yellow paint you'd need sunglasses to look at properly, I'd be concerned that it was a danger. There's nothing they'd be able to do to remove the step, it's inherent to the layout. As I pay for the meal, I ask the waitress if that kind of thing happens often. She admits that it's a fairly regular occurrence. One day, I guess some idiot will take a tumble and have the place shut down with an outrageous compensation claim.

Behind the café is a spectacular view across the harbour, and we head down a long flight of stone stairs for a closer look. We find a second hand Christian bookshop and a bright pink guest house, where Clem takes a dump and unfortunately gets some caught in the fur around her backside. This results in an embarrassing display (for all of us) where I have to put on a latex glove and use a wet wipe to clear up the mess as best I can. Once that lot is bagged up and disposed of, we can enjoy the views across the harbour. I take a few photos and my attention is caught by a huge seagull walking around on top of a parked car. I get closer and arse about with the aperture settings on the camera, by which time a second gull has barged aside the first and is now waiting for his close up. I oblige and it seems very happy with the attention.

We continue a slow walk around the town, popping into the Tourist Information office and a couple of gift shops. We see a little tourist card for sale, painted with a cartoon titled 'The Seasons of Skye'. There are 4 panels, one for each season, and it's raining in 3 of them. In the 4th, Winter, it's snowing.

I really like Portree, it has pretty much everything you could ask for in a town this small, and it's right next to the coast with some spectacular views. We reach the square and I give Clem another wipe down before letting her into the van.

Much of the afternoon is spent driving the loop around the northern part of the

island, the Trotternish Peninsula. The scenery, despite the awful weather, is stunning. It's entirely reasonable to suggest that the landscape could be considered amongst some of the finest on Earth, and although it would certainly be more photogenic were the sun out, the dismal conditions add an additional layer of wildness, a dimension of bleakness and isolation. It makes it more of an adventure.

We drive alongside the wonderfully named Loch Snizort and head for Uig, a pretty little village of less than 300 inhabitants. Its name derives from the Old Norse word for 'inlet', and was once in the hands of the Vikings. The approach is marked by a view looking down onto the harbour, where we stop to take a few photos. Opposite the huge white Uig Hotel is a small, cylindrical stone chapel, with an even tinier outbuilding next to it. The website for the Uig Hotel features the chapel as its main image on the homepage, no doubt confusing potential guests into believing that it's a very small hotel indeed.

On the other side of the village, the road ascends towards the heavens, and curls back on itself to reveal an amazing view down onto the village and the loch. The white houses scattered here and there look very pretty, nestled into the landscape, and it's almost impossible to believe that it feels like a megalopolis compared to what we are about to encounter.

Following the coast (it's hard not to on an island this small), we drive into a bleak and barren wilderness, with views across the frigid Little Minch towards the distant, and even more remote Western Isles. There are clusters of white houses in an otherwise empty landscape, an ocean of cropped, pale green grass with thicker tufts of dark green growth. It looks utterly at the mercy of the wind, and totally without warmth. And this is the Summer! Life looks as though it would be tough here, and you'd have to be a durable sort of person to exist without going mad. In Winter, under a layer of thick snow, it would look devastatingly beautiful but you'd be completely cut off from the world. That's pretty much the case even at the best of times.

Apart from the green, the white and the grey there is no other colour. Not even a flower.

We pass through a few tiny villages and I find myself wondering how on earth people make a living this far north. Fishing undoubtedly plays a large part in the local economy, but what else could they possibly get up to? Do people think differently about money up here? Everyone has bills and mortgages to pay – how on earth do they manage it? It gets me on a train of thought that will quickly formulate into an idea for a short story. As a writer, people sometimes ask where I get ideas from, and there is one of the answers – it starts with a question.

One thing they're not short of here is white paint. Nearly every building on Skye seems to be liberally coated with the stuff. Logically, one would think that every outer wall would be painted black, as a way of attracting and retaining the limited amounts of sunlight and heat, but clearly my understanding of science is not as good as that of the islanders, who after generations of living up here surely know best. An idle scan of the internet reveals that I'm not the only person to wonder about this, and the 'resolved question' response to this question is 'The Scots are skinflints, and whitewash is cheap.' I'm pretty sure that's not the real reason but it's all I could find.

A very small number of houses have left patches of stone to show through, where they either ran out of paint or prefer to rock the 'Dalmation' look.

The road narrows into a singletrack, and becomes interspersed with numerous passing places. We begin to see sheep wandering across the tarmac, and have to slow down for them to get out of the way. They nearly always look at our approaching van with curiosity, then suspicion, and when they finally realise we're going to keep going they make a comical dash for the verges. Clem is standing with her paws on the dashboard, her tail wagging furiously. Steph struggles to hold her still.

The mountains encroach to the verge on our right hand side, and the sea is off to our left. The thin ribbon of grey winds through the rugged landscape. Although much of the mountainous terrain is covered in a thin veneer of grass, there are huge gouges where the

granite shows through. By the rocky escarpments sloping to the very edge of the road, it seems that these mountains have a certain instability built into them, and every now and then a section collapses.

The sheep, of which there are plenty scattered about, don't seem to mind where they roam. We see a couple negotiating their way halfway up a mountain, and one stands on a rocky ledge, about fifty feet up, eyeing it's domain in a dumb silence.

We come to an odd little display shortly afterwards, and the clothes worn by those already here provide a riot of colour amongst the bleak scenery. Between the road and the sea is an outcrop of large boulders, and on top of these are hundreds of man-made miniature cairns. It's an arresting sight, and certainly very unusual. We park Sally and get out for a closer look.

We already recognise a few of the people from our short stay on the island. They are all bewitched by the display, and a few are taking photos. I grab my camera and start snapping away, and Steph starts making a little cairn of her own.

The biggest are about a foot in height and are made up from a dozen or so stones. They are surrounded by even smaller collections, some of which have about three stones, perhaps the minimum number required to

legitimately be called a cairn. Some have been built in the most inaccessible places, on the most distant boulders nearest to the sea. It must have taken quite some effort and determination to erect the furthest ones.

It's an inventive example of the human ability to create, and, as far as I can tell, completely pointless. Maybe that's why I like it so much. I haven't been able to find out why this place exists, or who started it, or even how long it's been there. Frankly, I'm amazed that the wind doesn't bring down the lot, but maybe it does. Maybe the whole display collapses in the fiercest gales and has to be rebuilt from scratch.

The road to Staffin provides us with even bleaker scenery, if such a thing were possible. Less houses, just green and grey, a world barely touched by man's presence. Inland, we see the Quirang, the result of various landslides as sections of the Trotternish Ridge range of mountains collapsed, thousands of years ago, leaving behind pinnacles and crags that are revered by walkers. Landmarks include the Table, the Needle and the Prison, all of which provide startling and almost unnatural shapes on the horizon.

I spot an abandoned building on the top of a hill and park up to go and investigate. With a howling wind and the rain lashing down, Steph opts to stay in the van with Clem, who is very settled

on her lap. I climb the hill, which turns out to be far bigger than I thought (and liberally sprinkled with sheep shit). I'm battered and soaked by the elements, but it's worth the effort. At the top, the roofless building at least offers some respite from the wind, so much so that I find myself surrounded by a kind of eerie silence.

I turn and take a photo of the van. In the distance, the ridges of the Quirang reach up to tear the underbelly of the sky. Far, far below, the road looks like a pencil squiggle. The van, bright orange and the only spot of warm colour in the entire, epic vista, is about the size of a tic-tac.

The inside of the building looks like a fly-tipping area, with bundles of steel wire, a few rotting wooden posts and some abandoned building materials. It must have been a horrible job bringing that lot all the way up here. On the other side, I step out onto the edge of a cliff, and look down hundreds of feet onto a windswept, steel-grey sea. Two needle-shaped rock formations lie just off the coast, the surf breaking against them in a plume of white spray.

Back at the van, I ask Steph where she thinks we should go next. I'm toying with the idea of cutting across the island and heading for Dunvegan, but the weather outside seems to be deteriorating yet further. We wonder what the point of staying on Skye would be, seeing as the rest of our time would probably amount to looking out at cold scenery between flashes of windscreen wiper blade. With a limited amount of time, the decision to stay rests on the chances of the weather getting better, and even hoping for a bit of sunshine. Clearly that isn't going to happen anytime soon.

We decide to leave.

Kyle of Lochalsh - Balmacara

We drive back through Portree, past our campsite at Sligachan, through Sconser and Broadford. We pass the Gypsies in the laybys and shortly after turn off towards the Kyle of Lochalsh. Although we're pushing it for time, we're still hoping to see Eilean Donan Castle in daylight.

It's a lot quicker getting off the island than it was getting on, and far more boring. We drive across the Skye Bridge, which is smaller than I'd hoped, and although I get Steph to take a couple of photos through the blur of the windscreen wipers, it's hardly worth it. It's only once we're over and briefly parked up half a mile down the road that the bridge becomes more of a spectacle.

Back on the mainland, the castle is less than ten miles away and the light is fading. We pass a campsite next to a hotel in Balmacara and discuss coming back this way if there's nowhere to camp by the castle. Not long after, the castle comes into view, a squat building that looks nothing like the photos we've seen. I've actually been here before, and I don't remember it as being this dull. Like most things, however, it has a good side, and we only see this once we're in the otherwise empty visitor car park.

From this angle, the view is stunning. The castle sits on a promontory of greeny-grey rock, surrounded by water with a backdrop of forest covered hills. I take a couple of pictures with the van parked in the foreground. The light conditions are by now pretty poor, and I think we'd be better off coming back in the morning for another go. If they allow dogs, we can go inside and take a look around.

There is a campsite close by, but it's fairly grotty and we don't fancy it. The clincher comes when we find out that we'd have quite a walk to the nearest pub. We head back to Balmacara through the hammering rain and arrive just as darkness is falling.

A sign tells us to park up and knock at the Warden's house, a whitewashed building behind a little fence at the back of the site. We open the gate and as we walk down the path we can see a man through the window, sitting at a table and eating his dinner. We briefly wonder whether we should give him a chance to finish and come back later, but decide to knock anyway. It seems rude, somehow, but the sign is pretty insistent that we don't set up on a pitch until we've seen the warden. He invites us into the conservatory and produces some paperwork, and makes a joke about being used to interruptions at dinnertime. We pay and he wishes us a nice stay.

The rain is lashing down, and neither of us fancies dealing with the van just yet. Steph wants a beer, I want a coffee, and we both want to sit somewhere warm and get out of our wet coats. We don't even bother hooking up to the electric.

Even though the hotel is about a hundred metres away, by the time we get there we're thoroughly soaked. Bedraggled and dripping, I enter what turns out to be a posh restaurant filled with well tailored diners. A few heads turn and look me up and down, this creature dripping on the hardwood flooring. It's a little bit like entering the 'Slaughtered Lamb'. A waiter rushes over to see what I'm doing here.

'Will it be OK to bring a dog in?' I ask, smiling. I already know the answer, and I can feel my hopes of getting warm sliding through the soles of my boots. There's no way he's going to let us in this place and risk a wet dog shaking itself all over the décor (and people's food). Even before he opens is mouth, I know he's going to send me back out into the cold, and I consider dropping to my knees and begging for just ten minutes in a warm corner, somewhere out of view.

'I'm sorry,' he says. 'The restaurant doesn't allow dogs, but you're welcome to go to our bar, which is around the other side of the building.'

A bar! Warmth beckons. I thank him and go back outside to relay the news to Steph. Based on the grandness and opulence of the restaurant, I imagine that the bar is going to be a smart and well-furnished cosy little hideaway, a retreat for the hotel guests to sit down on plush leather sofas and spend the night drinking cocktails. I couldn't have been more wrong. It's like the inside of a working men's club, a sort of annexe where they ran out of budget for the decor. Four surly geezers sit on stools next to the bar but the place is otherwise empty. I wonder if they're fishermen, back on shore for a break. A wall-mounted tv is showing some crappy programme or other, the sound just background noise. It doesn't feel that warm in here, and that includes the reception. The barman looks relatively happy to see us, at least until I appear to shock him by ordering a coffee and a large glass of Pinot Grigio, which he has to go into the main hotel to fetch.

We sit down on a bench by the radiator and peel off our coats. Clem, a bundle of wet fur, jumps up and we attempt to get her down but she's not having any of it. Our drinks arrive and we sit in silence for a little while whilst we write our journals. Within a few minutes, Clem starts getting restless. She's been an utter darling all holiday, quietly sitting and sleeping in Steph's lap as we've racked up the miles, but something seems to have gotten into her because she's up and down from the bench and doing her best to tangle the lead up amongst the table legs. Being terribly friendly, she keeps trying to make her way across the bar to the men at the bar, who are showing zero interest. I decide to take her outside and see if she wants a wee.

I put my wet coat back on and head back out into the wind and rain, which is steadily worsening. It takes about ten attempts to light a cigarette, by which time Clem has decided that she really doesn't want to be outside after all and is straining at the lead to get back in. Well, she'll have to wait. Not too long though, as it's so miserable out here I find myself trying to smoke a drooping stick of wet tobacco and drop it in disgust.

Tomorrow, Steph wants to go to Loch Ness. Originally, I'd planned on driving around northern Scotland, heading up to John O'Groats and coming back down through places like Wick and Thurso, but that would add another 400 miles to the trip and would waste at least an entire day. No offense to the locals but there's fuck all up there anyway.

No. We'll go to Loch Ness, and then through Inverness, which will be our most northerly point on the trip.

After a couple of drinks, there's no avoiding the inevitable return to the van and the rigmarole of configuring it for the night setup. As we step outside the bar, we're greeted by a hurricane. Rain sheets down and the howling wind shakes the nearby trees. It feels perfectly fitting for this part of the world. I wonder what it must be like at sea right now, and feel sorry for the poor bastards out riding the swells. They must be used to it, I guess, just another part of the daily struggle this far north.

We run back to the van but it doesn't prevent us getting another thorough soaking. I open the side door and Steph and Clem clamber inside whilst I dig out the electric cable from the underseat storage and connect us to the supply. I'd rather not put the roof up in this kind of weather, and nearly don't, but figure that the few trees scattered about the campsite will provide enough shelter to break up the wind a little. Besides, without the roof being up, there'd be nowhere to store the crates, resulting in us being unable to extend the bed.

Whilst Steph sits in the passenger seat, out of the way with Clem on her lap, I methodically go through the process of putting up the roof and moving the crates. I set up the table and turn on the heater. After about twenty minutes, we're sitting at the table with the portable convector heater pointed at us on full blast. It's been a very long and very wet day.

But it isn't over yet. We still have to brush our teeth and have a wash before hitting the sack, which means going outside and getting soaked again.

At some point during the night, I find myself awake and unable to sleep. At such times, I find that simply lying there and trying something as banal as counting sheep generally results in me still being awake half an hour later, with a count of three thousand, and in addition to being wide awake I'll also be angry at the entirely stupid idea.

I get up, get dressed and head outside for a smoke. The rain has ceased, albeit temporarily. Ten minutes from now, it will be hammering down, but for this short time I am witness to an amazing sight. The sky is a deep, rich blue-black colour and only a few thick cumulus clouds remain. A new cloudbank is on its way in, and the dark, central mass is surrounded by a shining grey edge where it's thin enough for the moon to illuminate it from behind. Sometimes, the sky is an under appreciated wonder of nature.

But not tonight.

Not by me.

Highlands – Urquhart Castle – Loch Ness – Aviemore

I keep waking up in the night. Rain thrums at the roof of the van and, at some ungodly hour, I'm disturbed by water dripping down onto my face. I assume it's from condensation because we had the heater on earlier.

It's a restless night, uncomfortable and cold.

Imagine our surprise when we awake to glorious sunshine. Steph is ecstatic. She practically leaps out of bed and takes Clem for a walk. I get dressed and reconfigure the van. By the time I'm done, it's raining again.

I change into some clean clothes. I only brought one fleecy jumper so I'm forced to put that back on. It feels cold and clammy. Everything is damp. As the days go by, and the rain continues to relentlessly fall from the sky, our whole world is getting damp and dirty – coats, curtains, clothes just don't get a chance to dry out.

When I nip out to the loo, even my fresh trousers get wet. I can't feel too sorry for myself though – I've only had a few days in a campervan, and some people fought in World Wars and lived in sodden trenches for years.

I snaffle down some cereal for breakfast and brew up coffee. The sun comes back out again, obviously playing Peepo! It changes everything. The Scotland we've seen has some impressive sights, but the incessant bad weather has really taken the shine off it. When the sun's out, and the views recede into the distance, Scotland is easily one of the most beautiful countries on Earth. I might keep mentioning this, but it's true.

At Eilean Donan Castle, things look very different from last night. The car park is chock full and we have to find a spot in the separate coach park, nestling in between a couple of huge coaches.

There's no way I'm going to be able to replicate the photo of the van in front of the castle, so I do what I can whilst Steph wanders inside the gift shop to ask if dogs are allowed. She returns a few minutes later with a negative response.

'Well, do you want to go and have a look whilst I wait?' I ask.

She shrugs. 'Not really.'

Although I could leave them behind and go inside to have a look around the castle, meaning I have once again abandoned them whilst I'm off doing my own thing, the thornier problem I'm faced with is rather more abstract. As this trip will eventually emerge as a book, am I obliged to go inside for the sake of the readers? Am I going to get a negative review from some person who takes great objection to the fact that I am, right now, standing outside one of Scotland's premier tourist spots, and won't even perform my writerly duty of traipsing around and describing what's inside? For those of you that think writing a book is easy, it isn't all Pimm's and sunshine.

I decide not to go inside the castle. Having since looked it up online, it was the right decision. It's not really a castle, more of a house, and if I was forced to look inside every single house we see I'd still be in Scotland now. I settle for a quick look inside the gift shop, and get a couple of pennies pressed into Eilean Donan decorations.

We get back in the van and spend the better part of the morning driving up into the Highlands. A sign warns us that feral goats are on the loose, but we don't see any. The road hugs the shore of Loch Duich before heading up into the craggy, mountainous terrain of the Five Sisters, all of which are around a thousand metres in height. To repeat that in a slightly different way, that means each pile of stone is a kilometre tall, which is no small amount of stuff. The mountains on both sides are liberally sprinkled with waterfalls, glistening in the rare moments of sunshine like veins of silver in the granite. We pass by Loch Cluanie, blocked at its eastern end with a dam for a hydroelectric power station. A tiny river trickles out on the other side, which will grow in size and feed into Loch Dundreggan.

We drive along the side of Loch Ness until we reach Urquhart Castle, and park up to find that no dogs are allowed. The custodians also want to charge an extortionate price for us to walk down and see the ruins. I'll be happy enough with a decent photo, so I have a scout around to find a good vantage point. Now, I'm not saying that this is a deliberate ploy to make people pay the entry fee, but the entire wall running the length of the car park has been blocked off by hedges and trees – getting a simple photo proves nearly impossible. I walk to the top of the car park and find a large gate with a 'NO ENTRY' sign, so I can't even walk a few yards to a great spot overlooking the castle. Frustrated, I walk back along the hedges and find a place where I can stick my arm through the trees and take a picture.

As we drive away, on a road that overlooks the car park, I realise that I can park up and, with a little bit of climbing, can see the castle in all its glory. I take a photo of the castle, with Sally in the foreground and the loch in the background. There's even a rainbow to frame the view rather nicely.

We continue to Drumnadrochit and find a place to park up for a coffee.

TERRA FIRMA TRAVELS

There's a large fibreglass model of Nessie right outside, and Steph clambers on with Clem to pose for a photo. As we're sitting at one of the outdoor coffee tables, Steph notices the sign advertising boat tours and I don't need much persuading to go and buy some tickets. We then sit around waiting for the minibus to take us down for the start of the tour, in half an hour.

A group of tourists arrives, mooches around the gift shop and then buys tickets for the same tour as us. They stand around, bored, for a full 25 minutes and then, with just 2 minutes to go before the minibus arrives, they disappear.

A bearded, fifty-something man in a cap boards us onto the bus and we wait. This is George Edwards, skipper of the Nessie Hunter IV, who makes a living taking tourists out onto the loch. He wanders into the gift shop and returns with bad news – the other people who bought tickets have buggered off to visit Urquhart Castle, knowing full well that the tour begins at 4pm and they won't be back until at least 5pm. Basically, even though they knew we were waiting for the tour to start, they thought that we would be forced to wait for their return.

George asks us if we'd mind waiting another hour, and I explain that we need to be at Aviemore before dark, so waiting really isn't an option. He doesn't look very happy. I'm pretty sure he expected us to say that it wouldn't be a problem. But the scheduled tour starts at 4pm, which is far more convenient for us.

'OK, I'll just take you two,' he says, slamming the door.

We're driven down to the shore in a moody silence. George parks up, opens the minibus door and brusquely tells us to get on the boat.

We step aboard and he informs us that no dogs are allowed into the warm interior cabin. I later learn, when he's mellowed out a bit and in a more talkative mood, that this is because he once had a dog on board that pissed everywhere, and it went down through the floorboards and into the engine room, where it apparently stank for weeks.

He unties the rope, guns the engine

and we leave the jetty. Soon, we're out over the deep waters of Loch Ness. The wind creates choppy little swells, and a curtain of spray throws itself at us. For once, it isn't raining, and this makes the experience a lot more enjoyable.

I'm not going to lie and say that we aren't hoping for a glimpse of the creature. In the back of my mind, there's even a fragile, nebulous hope that I'll be the one to finally nail a decent photo of whatever it is out there. Everybody who visits Loch Ness must think the same kind of thing – today will be the day the mystery is solved!

I take lots of photos (on a hi-res setting so I can check them later for any small heads peering from the water) and a few video clips. We head out into the centre of the loch and travel south, and I'm pleased to find that we go right past Urquhart Castle and get the most spectacular views, even better than if we'd paid an entry fee and stood amongst the ruins.

George calls me inside the cabin, and I ask if Steph can come in if she carries Clem. He reluctantly agrees, and we're glad to be inside, away from the spray and the chilly wind. He points at a screen showing sonar readings, which apparently shows the flatness of the loch bed.

The freshwater loch is 227 metres deep, and the bottom is unusually flat, a result of the sediment settling over time. Lots of time. It's over 22 miles long and holds more water than every lake in England and Wales combined. It's not an isolated body of water, being fed by the River Oich and Loch Oich at the southern end and Loch Dochfour at the north. Today, we've already seen two rainbows arcing through the sky and ending on the surface waters.

George must be well used to the scenery by now and pays it little attention. He's more focussed on his instruments.

I ask if he's been doing the job long. Twenty six years, he tells me in a voice that resonates with authority. He's well known around these parts, and used to dealing with the more or less constant flow of newspapers, magazines and tv production companies, though he dislikes most of what they publish as sensationalist crap.

I tell him that I cycled through Scotland in 1997 and tried to get a meeting with another monster hunter based on the shore at Dores.

'Steve Feltham,' he says with a sour expression.

'That's the guy. I bet you two are always out for a beer and swapping stories?'

'I can't stand the man,' he says.

I try pressing him further but he won't say any more.

'Have you seen the monster?' I ask, changing tack.

'If you'd bothered to read the information sheets, you'll see that I took these pictures.'

He's a charmer, all right. He points to an oversized postcard with a series of photos showing something in the water. It'd be fair to say that it could be Nessie. It would also be fair to say that it could have been pretty much anything.

I later discover that the reason George dislikes the Dores-based monster hunter so much is because Steve Feltham discredited these photos by saying the creature depicted was probably a fibreglass hump previously used in a National Geographic documentary (which George had participated in). George also has no time for Adrian

Shine, a marine biologist based at Drumnadrochit who is also considered a leading authority on the monster. You would have thought that they would all be working together, but it seems that professional rivalry gets in the way.

'So, do you think it's a plesiosaur?' I ask.

His face curls up in disgust.

'It would have to be a very old one,' he says, failing to hide the contempt in his voice, 'as the first sighting was in 525AD.' He's clearly in no mood to suffer what he considers to be idiotic questions. I wonder if he's this curt with everyone, or whether it's just me because he doesn't really want to be out here knowing he'll have to come back out when the other group finally return. Maybe he's just tired of answering the same old questions for 26 years.

The monster first came to the attention of the nation with a news report in 1933, when the Inverness Courier published a story based on the sighting of some sort of dragon-like creature by a London visitor. The 'dragon' was walking across the road, heading back to the loch, with an animal in its jaws. Dinner. Letters from readers came pouring in, detailing sightings of their own.

That same year, a motorcyclist reported a near miss with the creature whilst enjoying an early morning pootle around the loch. Had he hit the beast, it would have been interesting to see the insurance claim form.

Such was the interest that the Secretary of State for Scotland made an official order to the police to protect the monster from any trophy hunting locals.

Numerous sightings followed, and there are plenty of photographs and video clips, all of them unsubstantiated as proof of a previously unknown creature residing in these waters. Perhaps the most famous is the head and neck picture, the 'surgeon's photograph' first published in the Daily Mail in 1934. This was, however, exposed as a fake in 1979, and explained in great detail in a 1999 book. For forty-five years, the world had been fooled by a toy submarine with a wooden neck and head attached to it.

There have been numerous large scale expeditions over the years, all of them inconclusive. More than one expedition gathered proof of something (or things) in the loch, but the subsequent explanations range from seals, underwater logs, seismic gas bubbling to the surface through a fault in the loch bed (the gas is produced by rotting pinewood logs), and even the wind blowing water to one end of the loch and it re-establishing as a flat surface (an oddity known as a seiche).

Perhaps the most promising result, for those that want to believe, came from the Loch Ness Phenomena Investigation Bureau (LNPIB) study carried out between 1967-8. A device was fixed at Urquhart Bay and directed to the opposite shore, effectively forming a barrier across the entire loch. A number of 20ft long 'animate targets' were recorded moving from the depths and back again (but never surfacing). Professor D. Gordon Tucker, in charge of the equipment, decided that the objects were undoubtedly animalistic in nature, but not fish. He said: 'The high rate of ascent and descent makes it seem very unlikely that they could be fish, and biologists we have consulted cannot suggest what fish they might be.'

Whatever it was that Tucker thinks he found, it certainly wasn't the dopey looking creature in the Ted Danson film from 1996. If Nessie is an ancient predatory beast with a fondness for small children, it's more likely that sightings were actually of Jimmy Saville enjoying a swim (he had a house in Glencoe, not too far away).

George proffers a theory that the creature must be new to science and lists reasons why he believes it would be i) carnivorous, ii) must have gills and breathe water, iii) must be cold-blooded and iv) must be part of a breeding family.

'Some sort of fish,' he concludes, as though the matter has now been settled. All the way through the explanation, his voice has been flat, as though he'd been reading from a card. It's a well practiced argument, one I suspect he's recited, verbatim, thousands of times.

It's hard to see a flaw in what he's saying, as these conclusions are drawn from a logical starting point. They explain how such a creature – or creatures - can live in a relatively small loch and remain unseen.

'What about the SONAR equipment?' I ask.

He tells me that SONAR is no good for spotting the creatures, as it doesn't define shape. Visual camera systems are also useless as the loch is literally fogged up with silt. To illustrate, he lowers a small waterproof camera over the side and when the light is turned on all we can see is an underwater blizzard.

'Even on a good day, visibility is no more than a few feet,' he says, hoisting the camera back up.

Sunlight barely penetrates the surface layer of water. Consequently, there is very little algae or plankton in the loch, which George states is virtually devoid of any kind of life, with no more than about 30 tons of fish in the entire body of water.

'So you don't even think it could be a large sturgeon?' I ask.

'Pah!'

We are out in the centre of the loch, moving on a body of greyish water, surrounded by mountains. Even without the distraction of Nessie, it's a fantastic way of spending an hour or so. He turns the boat and steers it directly at the western shore, pointing out the display on the sonar screen as it shows the rising side of the bed. We head back towards the jetty, past Urquhart Castle again.

It doesn't look like today will be the day that a new discovery is made. We settle down and enjoy the ride, still unable to resist scanning the waters for any sign of a head. The boat thrusts through the water, and I wonder about the noise of the engine down below. Surely the noise would be uncomfortable for anything living under the water, and by now it would have learned to simply head the other way whenever a boat came by. In this day and age, I would have thought there'd be a better chance of finding the creature by positioning good-quality webcams around the shore and analysing each day's data with a computer.

We're soon back at the jetty and disembarking. I shake George's hand and thank him for the tour. He poses for a photo next to the boat and then shepherds us back onto the minibus. We thank him again when he drops us off, and clamber back into Sally.

Disappointingly, we're a few minutes late to get into the Loch Ness Exhibition at the Drumnadrochit Hotel (base of Adrian Shine), and we peer through the windows in the vain hope that somebody inside might take pity and let us in. No such luck.

Back at the van, another rainbow has appeared, arcing through the sky above Sally and disappearing into a field. Today is The Day of Rainbows.

We drive to (and through) Inverness, a lovely little city I remember well from my cycling trip. Back then, my friend J and I had spent two days cycling here from John O'Groats, which for a couple of unfit blokes was something of an achievement. On the third day, my body gave up and I couldn't negotiate the huge hill that leads out of town. I've been looking forward to seeing it again, if only to see if it actually was as bad as I remembered.

It's worse. The hill goes up a steep incline and seems to rise forever. Even the van struggles to climb it. After a day's rest at Inverness, J and I eventually managed to conquer it and continue with our trip, but I'm not so sure what would happen now if we were to undertake such a journey on bikes again. I've been toying with the idea of suggesting another trip to J for some time, but maybe motorbikes would be a better idea. He's even more unfit than I am now, fat and old with a dodgy knee. Age is a terrible thing.

It's 28 miles to Aviemore, through scenery that's mostly dull. We've been spoilt for spectacular views over the last few days and it had to end sometime. There's just nothing out here to look at. Not even a petrol station to offer a flash of colour.

We reach Aviemore in fading light. The town promotes itself as a tourist resort, and is popular with hill walkers and mountaineers, and skiers during the snowy depths of winter. During the 1960's, Prince Charles and Princess Anne came here to attend Royal Hunt Balls, and in the 70's the town played host to the 'It's a Christmas Knockout' tv show. In the late 90's, much of the old infrastructure was demolished but the promised rebuilding work never materialised. A short period of decline followed and when the new century began a conglomerate of private investors formed to rebuild and begin the process of attracting tourists once more.

Today, Aviemore looks and feels like a funky little town more suited to the Cornish peninsula. Steph says it reminds her of Jasper, Canada. The main drag features a long avenue of brightly lit shops and restaurants, B&B's and pubs. Hordes of young people walk around having a good time. A couple are dressed in board shorts – they must be freezing. Driving through in a VW Campervan, we add to the cliché and fit right in.

We drive around and check out a campsite a couple of miles out of town. It looks nice enough but Steph wants to be closer to the action. I suggest a B&B, thinking that at least we could have a few drinks and stagger back for a hot bath. I haven't showered in days. All part of the fun of touring in a campervan, of course, but I'm starting to feel a little grimy.

Back in the centre of town, the first B&B I try is empty. I go inside and ring the little bell but nobody comes. It's the Marie Celeste of boarding houses. The one next door doesn't allow dogs. A third is unsuitable – according to Steph, it 'looks like someone's house'. I thought they all did – isn't that kind of the point? Cold, tired and becoming increasingly frustrated with all the messing about, I think that I can at least get something accomplished by putting some petrol into the van. By the time Sally's had her fill, we haven't got enough money left for a decent B&B anyway.

I start driving back towards the campsite and, right at the end of the main drag, we see a pizza parlour and a previously missed sign for a different campsite. Holy moly, this is exactly what we've been looking for. I waste no time in checking us in. For the fantastic price of just £17, we get a pitch and electric hookup, and use of some of the best campsite facilities I've ever seen. Bargain!

It is the darkest campsite I've ever seen as well though, and the pitches are really hard to make out. I'm not joking when I say that the guy a couple of pitches up from us actually drives his own campervan into a tree whilst manoeuvring into position. I carefully reverse onto our pitch and faff about with the electric hookup. By the time I've got the crates out of the back I'm literally shaking with cold. Steph stays inside with Clem, sorted for light and heat, whilst I head down to the pizza parlour and order pizzas, salad and the inevitable bottle of Irn Bru one has to at least sample whilst in Scotland.

It's the law.

Pitlochry –
The Wallace Monument (Stirling) –
The Dunmore Pineapple –
The Falkirk Wheel

The campsite is dark and silent and we get a great night's sleep. Wake about 8am and Steph gets up to walk Clem whilst I unmake the bed and pack everything away. It's a relatively painless procedure this morning. I think I'm getting into a routine.

Not owning a campervan has proven to bring on a bit of culture shock each time we've hired one. They may look delightful but they aren't easy beasts to live in. Things take a lot of getting used to. There's a definite period of adjustment. Maybe I'm slow, but it takes until today before I feel the final barriers crumble and things become normal.

The weather hasn't helped, keeping the environment cold and damp. But the main hurdles seem to be over. It's a pity we only have a couple more days with Sally. Still, the last time we hired a van it took almost a full two weeks before I was happy, so this is definitely an improvement. Steph, however, loves the idea of owning a campervan, despite the obvious discomforts.

Before setting off, we tend to our ablutions. The campsite facilities here are brilliant. We have a pass key that lets us into a separate block, which is warm and airy, clean and well stocked. Plenty of toilets and showers, a laundry room, vending machines, and even a condom machine and a wall-mounted box that sells lighters with the campsite logo printed on them.

As I come back outside, I see a guy getting his RV ready to leave the site. I wander over and say hello, and waste no time in asking if I can have a look through his windows. He answers my request with a hard, suspicious look. Why on earth would I be asking to look through his windows?

'I'm in a little campervan down there,' I explain, 'and I've been living like a hunchback for a week. I wouldn't mind a glimpse of Paradise for a moment.'

I realise that saying this has probably

just offended a small number of people who have bought this book mainly on account of their love for campervans. RV's are, to many people, the scourge of modern travel, even more despised than caravans. Well, maybe not quite. There's a sort of inverted snobbery attached to RV's, in that the people driving around in them aren't really travellers, more like pottering pensioners. Somehow, VW's and the like have a status of being the 'real deal', whereas huge RV's are to be pitied.

I disagree. RV's are ace. Plenty of room, all the mod cons, air conditioning, beds you don't have to deconstruct every morning. But what they gain in comfort – and they do look really comfortable – they lose in manoeuvrability and road practicality. They might be perfect for cooking and sleeping in, a veritable home from home, but getting around can be a bugger. It must be a nightmare trying to negotiate some of the smaller towns and cities, particularly in heavy traffic. Of course, the very thought of it being a home away from home is offensive to some purists, who think that if you go on the road in such comfort you might just as well have stayed at home in the first place.

Far from telling me to piss off and stop being so damned nosy, the man invites me inside. I clamber up the steps and say hello to his wife, sitting and looking bemused at some stranger walking into her lounge. They have a dog, a lovely golden lab, and he gets a lot of fuss. So much fuss, in fact, that I almost forget that I wanted a look at the inside of the RV.

It's as palatial as I expected – huge interior, lounge, bedroom with en-suite facilities, a massive fridge-freezer, plenty of storage etc. The one thing that's missing, and I find this wonderful, is the obligatory tv set. They don't have one, preferring to read and play board games instead.

I ask how easy it is to manoeuvre something this size and he confirms my thoughts, that it's a breeze until you get to more populated areas. Narrow city streets are a problem, as are supermarket car parks. The man tells his wife that I'm staying in a VW campervan and she says that she envies us.

The thing is, she's absolutely right – if I were forced to make a choice about which vehicle to take on a tourist trip, I'd still pick the campervan, despite all the issues we've had. It's a nice surprise to thank them and then walk away, back to Sally, and find that I don't really envy them at all. Ten minutes ago, I'd have thought the idea absurd, and despite a tour of an amazing RV, and it being filled with all the things I've been missing for the last week or so, and despite it confirming my thought that RV's are spacious and idyllic, I'm still drawn back to the VW.

I suspect that were I older, and unable to cope with all the upheaval of reconfiguring the interior every day, my inclination will be to travel by RV, but until then I'll stick with the VW.

We drive towards Stirling, on a road that is flat and surrounded by rather boring countryside. At Dalwhinnie, there are mountains again and the scenery improves. I say improves, but it's driving along this stretch that it strikes me that although everything is present and correct for a gorgeous vista, there's something wrong. It takes a little while to work it out. On the surface, it reminds me a lot of Switzerland – there are mountains and lakes, with an undulating, winding road that takes us through it all in a way that would have been impossible a hundred years ago.

Any graphic designers reading this will know that graphic-orientated software packages have a thing called a filter, where certain changes can be applied to any picture. You can change a picture of a dog into a watercolour version, or a mosaic, or any number of preset results that you require. The scenery around these parts looks like Switzerland but with a 'horror filter' applied.

There are mountains, yes, but unlike the sun-baked, snowy-capped Swiss beauties, the Scottish mountains are grimmer, swathed in mist and their peaks are obscured by a fug of dismal grey cloud. The sparkling cobalt lakes of Switzerland are here reproduced in slate grey. The clean, crisp Continental roads are now dirty, pock-marked ribbons of misery. The emerald green swathes of Swiss countryside are here just brown and dark green scrub. Nothing glows in the radiance of a bright, hot sun. Bare patches of gravel are like hideous scars on the landscape. Ugly pylons march across the wilderness like sentinels of doom. It doesn't help that we're listening to a compilation of Nick Cave's greatest hits as we're driving through all this.

All this said, I love it. It can't all be fluffy bunnies and rainbows, and I'm one of those people that can get a certain perverse satisfaction out of misery. Driving through the outskirts of Mordor with 'The Weeping Song' at full blast sounds like Hell, but I'm actually quite enjoying myself.

I've cycled this part of Scotland, and I can definitely confirm that it's a lot more pleasant doing it in a warm campervan this time around.

We stop at Pitlochry, a place I have nice memories of, and park up in the High Street to get out, walk Clem and find a bite to eat. It's a pleasant enough spot for what it is (or rather what we see of it), a shop-lined main street heading downhill and plenty of people walking around in winter clothing. We take our food back to the van and settle in for 10 minutes to wallop it down. Sandwiches, hot coffee and ice cream, pretty much the perfect snack.

We're parked on the end of a line of cars, the last available spot before the double yellow no parking lines begin. About halfway through our food, a small van parks right in front of us, so tight to the bumper that it'll be impossible for us to drive away when we've finished eating. A man rushes off and leaves his wife to lock up. I get out of the van and ask her how long they'll be parked there.

Her face scrunches up in disgust and anger. She reacts as though I told her I've just murdered their cat. Before I have a chance to explain that I'm only asking because we're leaving shortly and after we've gone they can have our space, she's jabbing her finger in my direction giving me a round of fucks and asking what it's got to do with me how long they're going to be parked there.

Well! Somebody missed a day at anger management class. To be fair, I'm not the best at handling people with such idiotic tendencies. I know the NLP techniques for creating empathy and bringing such people down to a level of calmness but sometimes it's just not worth the effort. I tell her to shift her van as she's blocked me in, and this pushes the level of abuse up another notch, and the commotion attracts her husband, who runs back to the van with a red face.

He calms down his wife and asks me what's going on and I tell him we're about to leave soon and he's blocking us in. He explains that he's just unloading some gear into his shop and would we mind waiting another 5 minutes?

'No problem,' I say.

He grabs some stuff from the boot and walks away. The woman glares at me. I give her my sweetest smile and head back inside the van to finish eating. As it turns out, they take longer than 5 minutes but I use the extra time to look in a couple of shops and return to the van once they've driven off.

There's no mistaking the Wallace Monument. I thought it'd be a small block of carved granite on a plinth somewhere, but it's enormous. We first see it from miles away, a colossal sandstone pillar-shaped construction on top of Abbey Craig, a hill that overlooks Stirling (and pretty much everywhere else). Legend has it that William Wallace watched the English forces gather from this craggy vantage point before going on to defeat them at the battle of Stirling Bridge.

This is only a flying visit, so whilst Steph walks Clem around the car park I head on up to take a few photos. The walk up to the top of the hill is a killer, and I wish I'd waited for the shuttle bus. Still, the trail cuts through the forest and it's very easy to get lost in a little fantasy of thinking you're someone from a few centuries ago on their way to attack a hilltop fortress. Maybe it's just me, but I often find when visiting castles that I spend quite a bit of time wondering how to breach the defences. Not a wholly ridiculous endeavour when you realise that these kinds of buildings were built precisely for protecting people against attack. Each one is a logic puzzle.

At the top of the hill, I'm dwarfed by the monument. Built in the 19th Century and funded by public and foreign donations, it stands a further 220 feet higher than Abbey Craig and has a number of interior rooms containing artefacts purportedly from Wallace himself, including a five and a half feet Claymore sword, which would have been about as long as the average Scot was tall. Wallace was said to be a huge, burly man, with one account suggesting he was as much as 7ft in height. Although it doesn't adhere to historical fact across much of its running time, Braveheart does include numerous jokes about Gibson's height, an acknowledgement that screenwriter Randall Wallace (an American with Scottish roots) was well aware of the fabled size of Wallace.

I take a few pictures and head over to the viewing platform. There's a little plaque that has the distant mountains etched into it. From here, I can see Stirling Castle, the site of the battle, a great tract of the Forth Valley and the distant mountain of Ben Lomond (and numerous other 'Ben' mountains). On a clear day, even Loch Lomond is visible.

I head back down to the car park. After my visit, I discover that there used to be a statue of Wallace down here too, a 13ft sandstone monster that didn't rely on historical accounts for its depiction of Wallace, but used imagery taken from the movie. Essentially, it was a 13ft statue of Mel Gibson. Now, at the time of installation, Gibson was at the height of his popularity – this was long before the infamous 'sugar tits' outburst and other accusations that have seen his career take a somewhat downward trajectory of late. It's a sign, then, of how badly the film was received in Scotland that the statue became the subject of intense abuse. The Scotsman newspaper printed that it is 'amongst the most loathed pieces of art in Scotland' and an unnamed local was quoted as saying it is a 'piece of crap.' Not content enough to leave it at a few words of disgust, various unhappy characters physically attacked the statue, resulting in it being covered in paint, struck with a hammer and, most unnervingly, having its face gouged out.

You have to have some serious issues if you go out on a bitterly cold Scottish night and spend the early hours gouging out the face of a statue.

As can be guessed, it all ended badly, with the statue being removed after just 11 years of tumultuous display. The artist tried to sell it, and then found he couldn't even give it away, and it ended up back on display in his own studio.

We clamber back into the van and head off towards Airth, where a couple more interesting old buildings await us. The first is Dunmore Park House, a wreck of a building that is no longer in use and is worth a look around. Again, there's something very invigorating about seeing a grand building fallen into ruin, and it's very humbling to know that even something once doused in opulence can fall into neglect given enough time and lack of funding.

The GPS leads us to a dirt track and I begin driving down it. A couple of 'PRIVATE' signs do little to deter us (although Steph's not happy about ignoring them). After so far, it looks like we're approaching the grounds to someone's house, and I begin to think twice about carrying on. Dunmore Park House itself seems to be totally inaccessible, and our search ultimately takes us to a farm surrounded by a number of outbuildings and a thoroughly uninviting flooded mud track. Time to abandon our plan and focus on the Dunmore Pineapple instead.

A man approaches with his two dogs walking alongside, and I roll down the window and ask if he knows where the Pineapple actually is. He tells us to head back towards Airth and try one of the other tracks further along.

We've stopped at the only place where it's possible to turn the van around, and I thank the guy and head off the way we came. Back on the main road, we get a tantalising glimpse of the ruins of Dunmore Park House, but still find no way of accessing it. A half mile down the road there's another dirt track marked with 'PRIVATE' signage.

We drive down the track. It gets bumpier and muddier the further we go, but there's no way to turn around. Wherever we're going, we're committed to getting there. The track devolves into a muddy ribbon with a raised bank of grass in the centre. Twice I have to get out and check that there's enough clearance under Sally to continue. Thankfully there is, otherwise it would have meant reversing all the way back to the main road.

We negotiate our way through some monstrous puddles. Eventually, the track ends at a farmer's field.

'This can't be right.'

I check the GPS, on which the track continues to where we want to go. Bloody thing. I get out and walk a little while but it seems as though my route through a forest is taking me further from where I'm trying to get to. Ah, forget it. I walk back to the van, carry out a ten-point turn, and slowly drive back to the main road. I'm gutted – I really wanted to see both of these buildings.

We eventually rejoin the main road and reach Airth, where to our delight there's a brown National Trust sign pointing the way to the Dunmore Pineapple. After all this crawling about trying to be stealthy, the place actually welcomes visitors! We follow the signs and drive down a deteriorating narrow road to a dirt car park.

With Clem, we enter the grounds and find ourselves on a manicured lawn leading up a slight incline to a spectacular old building with an enormous concrete pineapple on top of it. It's quite a sight, and worth all the trouble it's taken to get here. The main building is oblong shaped, with great walls extending on either side, covered with ivy and wildflowers. It looks like something from a children's book.

We're not alone. Another couple are walking around the grounds with their unleashed monster of a greyhound. It's as big as a horse, and suddenly comes bounding towards me at incredible speed. Jeezo, it's terrifying. It turns at the last minute and races around the garden, and Steph struggles to hold Clem back from chasing after it. Quite what she'd do if she ever caught it is another matter, but I wouldn't be

surprised if she was snaffled up and swallowed before she even had a chance to realise what was happening.

They wander off and we're left to enjoy the place alone. I take a dozen photos and some close-ups of the wildflowers against the walls. On either side of the pineapple cuppola and the vestibule beneath it, quarters for the gardeners appear used and lived in. We can see a half full bottle of washing up liquid on one of the windowsills. The Landmark Trust rents the place out as a holiday cottage and it's certainly one of the most impressive holiday lets I've ever seen.

The obvious question to ask is why on earth would anybody build a house and then put a huge concrete pineapple on top of it.

John Murray, the 4th Earl of Dunmore, had the place built as a birthday present to his wife, a garden retreat from which to view the grounds. So far, so logical. But why the pineapple?

The exact reason is unknown. However, the entire building is essentially a folly, and the whole point of a folly is to give the world a show of ostentation, an often pointless and vulgar advertisement to the world at large that someone is doing very well in life.

At the time of building, pineapples were a luxurious commodity (some would say that they probably still are in Scotland), and the inclusion of an elaborately designed, ginormous concrete pineapple is perhaps a double-display of ostentation, a great big 'Fuck You' to the idea of being conservative and frugal. All across Europe, the pineapple motif was worked into stone, wood and iron, and represented a generic symbol of wealth and power.

Although one might think that a massive stone pineapple was the result of a moment of whimsical madness, or the loss of a particularly strange bet, the execution of the building work and design suggests that a great deal of thought went into the project. Each individual leaf is designed to channel away rainwater, and at no point does water have a chance to accumulate and freeze, thus damaging the stonework.

It might seem incredulous to readers of a modern disposition and outlook that a building this size based on a pineapple ever came to fruition, but consider that even now there stands a thoroughly modern building in central London that has become known as the 'Gherkin'.

Steph tries one of the three doors in the porch of the main building. Unsurprisingly, they're all locked. I know why she tried though – it would have been even more amazing to go inside and see what the interior looked like.

We walk along the massive wall and find a gap. Many estates have walled gardens, not only for privacy but also to provide more advantageous conditions for fruiting crops – the ground enveloped by the walls is less susceptible to frost and can even form a kind of microclimate where non-

indigenous, exotic fruits can prosper. Walled gardens make it possible to cultivate vineyards this far north of the equator.

We find ourselves in a thin band of forest looking out onto a ploughed field. In the distance, I can see the Dunmore Park House ruins again. It looks like it'd be at least an hour for a round trip, and that'd be slogging our way through plenty of mud. I ask Steph if she fancies it. She doesn't. It's getting late and she is ready to head off towards Edinburgh. She wants a bath, which clearly isn't going to happen unless we get a B&B. She also wants somewhere she can watch the X-Factor, which I'm against on general principle.

Quite how a bunch of talentless arseholes singing glorified karaoke became a national institution I'll never know. It's part of the general malaise eating away at society, where everybody thinks they deserve to be famous. Nowadays, people think it's enough that you can sing in the shower – if you mom overhears you and tells you how good you are, it's time to audition for the X-Factor and prepare yourself for playing stadiums. The entire entertainment industry is being taken away from the truly creative people, the ones who'd never go on a tv talent show even with a gun to their head.

We set off for Edinburgh, but don't get very far before I see a sign for the Falkirk Wheel. I've heard about this place and think it's worth a short detour to go and see it.

It appears to be tucked away behind a grotty housing estate. We arrive to see the last of the staff walking back to their cars and operations closed for the day. I ask if we can see the wheel and the viewing area is still open, so we park the van and walk down for a look. You can see it on the approach but standing in front of it reveals the true scale and engineering genius that went into the build. It's amazing, a series of grey, ornately designed steel pillars that shrink in size as they encroach into a hill and fool the eye into seeing a skewed perspective. The two pillars nearest us feature a section that is essentially a huge bath, on which barges float whilst they are hoisted into the sky.

Until the 1930's, Edinburgh and Glasgow were connected by two canals, the Forth and Clyde and the Union. They linked together via a series of 11 locks, which gradually fell into disrepair (which, from all the buildings we've seen on this trip, is surprisingly easy to allow – we may even see the 'Gherkin' crowned with Kudzu vines in our lifetimes). These locks were eventually filled in and incorporated into the land, forever severing the link. When British Waterways decided to implement a regeneration plan (with support and funding from numerous partners, including the Millennium Commission), they invited designs for a boat-lift to represent Scotland's prosperity into the 21st Century, and the colossal structure that stands before us was the eventual winner.

As a way of connecting two canals separated by a height of 80ft, it's a deceptively simple and aesthetically pleasing design. I'd go so far as to say 'beautiful', and it has an elegance that belies it's role as a powerhouse of functionality. If only the rest of the world were as well designed as some of the places we've seen on this trip, it would be a far more interesting and wonderful place to live in.

The fact that we are here alone, and

also because the mechanism is dormant, lends the environment an abandoned air, and I get the same feelings of isolation and an intrusion of thoughts of a post-Apocalyptic nature that I get when visiting modern ruins or underground installations. It's fantastic, and I spend a few idle moments wondering what the world would be like if there were only pockets of survivors and places like this were to remain dormant forever, slowly rusting into decay. Look on my works, ye mighty and despair. The men who built this are no more. All is ruin.

Steph has discovered a little adventure playground and calls me over to witness her coming down a slide with Clem in her lap. At first I think it's an odd place for a collection of swings and slides but after a few moments it makes perfect sense. There are also burger vans and an ice cream stall (unfortunately closed). There's a visitor gift shop and plenty of space for coaches.

This place isn't just a link between canals, it's a social hub. People don't just come here to move barges around, they also come to look at this magnificent piece of machinery. It's a spectacle of entertainment just as much as it is a practical solution to an awkward problem. There are picnic tables. People eat ice creams and burgers and their children play on the slides.

But not today.

Forth Bridge –
Fife Coast Tourist Route -
Pettycur

The M9 takes us to Edinburgh but I turn off at the last minute and head across the Forth Bridge. Part of the reason for doing this is simply because I want to drive over it. In the fading light, it looks beautiful – two great columns heading up into the darkening sky, the graceful curve of the bridge itself. On the approach, you can't see the river far below, and it gives the impression of driving over a vast chasm. That's too good to drive past.

The other reason is that I don't want to start messing about looking for B&B's in a city centre during rush hour. Although it's a Saturday, traffic is horrendous as shoppers and staff make their exodus from the city. The thought of spending the next few hours in gridlock isn't at all appealing. I know from bitter experience that even though our requirements are relatively simple – a B&B, clean and basic with a charge of about £60 for the night, that allows dogs, is within walking distance to a nice pub, has a bath and a tv set, and also has safe parking – big cities rarely deliver the goods without aeons of pissing about. Far better, I think, to cross the bridge and follow the Fife Coast Tourist Route, where we will surely be inundated with very pleasant and homely establishments that will give us everything we want.

From the words alone - Fife Coast Tourist Route – we imagine that we'll pass through some delightful scenery dotted with B&B's just waiting for tired tourists to be given a hearty welcome.

After crossing the bridge, we find ourselves in a kind of industrialised zone that surely wouldn't attract even the most lunatic of tourists.

Just after Dalgety Bay we see a lovely looking hotel, which we drive past under the assumption that it'll be far more expensive than a B&B. After another few miles of seeing nothing whatsoever in the way of accommodation, we decide to bite the financial bullet and turn the van around. What we didn't notice as we initially passed the hotel was the number of vehicles parked outside, mostly on double yellow lines. There's also a mobile disco van, and a closer look through the hotel windows reveals that the place is packed with revellers celebrating a wedding. There's no chance of getting a room, and even if they could squeeze us into a broom cupboard it's likely we'd be kept awake all night by shite 70's disco, and hordes of pissed people screaming 'Come On Eileen!' until dawn.

We carry on. The next three hotels we find are all similarly packed with wedding guests, each celebrating the nuptials of whoever got married today. Which looks like half the city of Edinburgh. We couldn't have picked a worse night to try and find accommodation.

We eventually spot a holiday park and decide to stay there. We're getting sick of driving around in the dark. I pull in and park up by the Reception area. Steph and Clem wait in the van as I go inside to find no staff and no discernible Reception. I speak to a couple of elderly zombies bumbling their way around in a stupor and they tell me that nobody's here after 5pm.

'What's the point of that?!' I scream at them, spraying their wrinkly old faces with spit. Actually, I don't. I thank them and shuffle out back to the van.

'Well?' asks Steph, her voice loaded with hope that we'll soon be parked up with the heater on.

'Not a chance,' I say.

We agree that if we can't find a B&B within the next half hour we'll come back here and, come what may, spend another night in the damp van, even if it means staying in the damned car park. Needless to say, any further searching proves fruitless. We drive on into the darkness, occasionally interrupted by some tired, disintegrating shorefront town on its last legs. One of these towns is so rundown that even the McSquitty's Bar signage offering 'ALL DRINKS £2!!' wasn't enough to stop the place being closed down for good.

Some tourist trail this is! I've a good mind to sue the Tourist Board for fraud, enticing us out here with their fancy signs and giving us nothing but warehouses, boarded up towns and wedding parties.

We forget about any idea of getting a room in a dry, warm building and turn back to drive to the camp. It's the most enormous holiday park I've ever seen. Hill after hill loaded with static caravans and chalets, with nary a spare inch of ground between them. This is holiday parking for the masses, the Easy Jet of the caravan holiday world. On and on it goes, miles before we find ourselves approaching the entrance.

'There's no way we'll get a spot here,' I say, my brain slowly turning to mush at the thought of driving back to Edinburgh and starting our search from scratch.

'What about that place?' asks Steph.

Well, if there isn't a smaller caravan park opposite the monstrous one. I pull in and barely make it to the entrance gate before we see a sign saying 'NO TOURERS'. Bastards. I turn around, cross the road and enter the big site. We spot a sign telling overnighters to go along a small track alongside the road. At the end of it is a car park with a couple of RV's and some smaller touring caravans. The ground is littered with muddy puddles.

'We'll stay here,' I say. Steph smiles, accepting defeat. No bath and no X-Factor for her tonight.

Before parking up, we drive the short distance back to Kingham, where I nip into the local Costcutter for a jar of coffee and some milk. The only thing worse than spending the night in a damp van in a dirty car park is waking up in the morning without any coffee to drink. Of course, being raped and murdered would actually be worse, but no coffee is probably next on the list. Suitably provisioned, we drive to the local chippy for a takeaway dinner.

I park up and lock the driver door, purely out of habit. A huge feller walking past stops to watch me. He's clearly pissed.

'No need to do that,' he says.

I thank him, not really understanding what he's talking about, and check I've locked the door.

'No need to lock your door,' he says. He looks offended. Angry even.

'Just fuck off and mind your own business,' I say.

You already know that I didn't say that.

'Really?' I say. He's standing there, swaying gently, expecting some sort of conversation. Eighteen stone of pissed lard is staring at me.

'Nobody will steal anything,' he says.

'Nice town is it, then?' I ask, hoping he'll just go away. I'm already pretty certain that it's a shithole, so asking the question seems a little redundant. Apologies, Kingham, for such a damning judgement but you've caught me at the end of a very exasperating evening.

'Yeah,' he says.

'OK then,' I say and walk off into the chip shop, hoping he doesn't follow me. Thankfully, he doesn't.

I'm greeted by an Eastern European man, silently consolidating his people's grip on the service industries of Scotland, and a younger Asian. I say greeted, but they don't really welcome me inside, just look at me and wait for me to speak.

'Chips, please. One large, one small. And a bottle of Irn Bru.'

Apart from a few chips in the warming hatch, the rest of the shop is empty. No sign of any fish, scallops (the potato variety) or sausages. Now I'm here I quite fancy a battered sausage. I ask if they have any. The younger guy says he can cook one up for me. I say no thanks, preferring not to wait around. I just want to grab the food and go.

'It's no trouble,' he insists.

'No, you're OK. Just the chips.'

'It'll take 4 minutes. Go on, have a sausage.'

Christ, I've encountered the Mrs Doyle of the sausage world.

'Nope, cheers.'

He asks where I'm from. I tell him. He says he once worked in Daventry, which he thinks is the same area but is actually nowhere near it. He then asks where I've been.

'All over Scotland. It's been raining all week.'

This elicits no response. He doesn't smile, just looks at me. I think my sausage refusal may have upset him. Suddenly, there's a bit of an awkward silence. I decide to fill it by talking crap.

'Yeah, been pissing down all week! Scotland, eh?'

This time, they both stand and stare at me, expressionless. It's all getting a bit weird. The older guy places two bags of chips onto the counter, then the Irn Bru.

'Four pounds ninety,' he says.

What?!? Normally, I'd question this kind of consumer mugging but this time I can't be bothered. I've had enough of the world today, I just want to park up and vegetate. I hand over a fiver. Even if I have been ripped off, as long as the chips are hot I won't come back and put the windows through later.

Back at the site (or rather the car park) we find a spot and settle in for the night. Once we're connected up to the electric supply, the lights go on, quickly followed by the heater. I set up the table and we open our bags of chips to see what grisliness awaits us. We're very relieved and pleasantly surprised to discover that the food is very decent, and still piping hot. There's still the obligatory 5% of manky bits, something all chip shops without fail feel the need to include, and a fair number of otherwise delicious chips containing those little black eye things – what the hell are they, anyway? – but on the whole it's a tasty supper. Supper being the correct word, as it's 10pm already.

We eat in a silence punctuated only by chomping and the occasional snort at a hot bit of potato. Clem watches us avidly, waiting for some castoffs.

Ahead, through the windscreen, we get a view of the inky Firth of Forth and the distant, twinkling lights coming from the coastal edges of Edinburgh. Despite most of the evening being a disappointing write-off, it crystallises nicely on this almost perfect moment, the sitting in a warm van, bellies full, gazing out across the dark waters at the garland of Edinburgh lights. Had we found a B&B or a hotel, we'd have missed this, and spent a couple of hours in a generic room with beige walls staring absent-mindedly at whatever crap was being spouted from the tv.

Although we were forced into staying here, it worked out for the best.

Edinburgh –
Berwick-Upon-Tweed

We wake at 8:30am and I reset the alarm so we can have a bit of a lie-in. Rain is hammering at the roof and there's a gale blowing. Another glorious day in Scotland. We snuggle under the duvet for an extra half-hour's warmth.

When we do finally get up, it's freezing. I quickly get dressed and trudge to the loos. The men's block is locked but there's a single toilet around the back, in a small room where the door is jammed open with a mop. It's a dismal room for a dismal business, and I end up pissing into a dirty toilet bowl with a garden hose hanging over one side. Jeezo.

Edinburgh, viewed across the Forth, is now a blurry grey coastline that looks thoroughly uninviting. We're going there today.

I go through the usual rigmarole of unmaking the bed and restoring all the crates in their hidey-holes. I'm hoping that we can simply drive off the site without paying. I would have paid, obviously, if I could have found the Reception area, or if the site had made any provision to make payment possible, but if it's this hard to give them money I'm happy to clear off without bothering. I'm a fucking outlaw, me. Fifteen years ago, I might even have gotten a little buzz out of 'doing a runner', but now it's

more a middle-aged view of 'Well, if they can't provide any decent facilities....'

As I'm taking a couple of photos and getting ready to leave, a little silver car pulls up and an elderly gent clambers out. He looks like an extra from 'Still Game', rheumy-eyed with a pinkish whiskey-nose. He introduces himself as the Warden. Damn. Five minutes earlier and we could have gotten away with it. I ask him how much we owe him and he says £22.

'Really?' I ask, genuinely shocked. 'You want £22 for a pitch that's just a car park with no facilities?'

He apologises profusely for the lack of amenities and as we start chatting he wins me over. I quite warm to him. His name is Ben and Saturday is his only night off, which is why he wasn't there last night when we arrived.

'If I didnae take the wife oot on a Saturday night I'd be divorced by noo!' he says, eyes twinkling. He apologises again, and even tries to apologise for the terrible weather.

'Been a cruel year for the weather,' he says. 'The owner reckons he's oot £3 million in lost custom.' He tells me a little more about the owner. 'There was nothing here, just hills that you couldnae even put sheep on. He put roads in and made all this.' He sweeps his arm to encompass the site. 'He's a millionaire, many times over.'

It's clear that he admires the guy. Even though I'd only consider the fee to be acceptable at £10, which is the same for a space at a motorway service station (with less puddles and more inviting facilities), I hand over the full amount. Not because I wanted to, because I could have demanded to see the owner and argued with him until the cows came home, but simply because I liked Ben. I didn't want him to suffer any grief when he was only doing his job. If the owner of the Pettycur Bay Holiday Park happens to read this, you have a wonderful ambassador for your campsite in Ben the Warden. Give him a big Christmas bonus.

'Have a safe trip home,' he says, shaking my hand and clambering back into his little silver car. He drives off, and we finish getting the van ready to leave.

We head back to the Forth Bridge along the same coastal road we drove along last night. In daylight, we can see that there are one or two pockets of scenic loveliness, but on the whole it's still a slightly depressing drive.

The rain really picks up as we approach the bridge, and there's a layer of low cloud obscuring the view. We cross, buffeted by strong gusts of wind and sheeting rain. Halfway over, I look to my left at the parallel railway bridge and see only a dim ghost of it, the main segments barely revealing themselves in the gloom. It's very eerie.

It's not far to Edinburgh, where the GPS immediately starts to send us the wrong way down a one-way street. The whole unnavigable mess is worsened by an endless series of roadworks and diversions and I begin to wonder if we'll ever find our way into the city centre. Eventually, though, we do. I'm led to believe that there are numerous car parks, evident by the symbols on the GPS screen and their real world counterpart signage. This said, upon nearing each car park the expected final signs would disappear and we'd be left wondering just what the hell was going on. I suspect that some of the car parks were little more than back streets without any yellow lines painted on them, but they were all full anyway.

'Is it us?' asks Steph at one point. 'Are we doing something wrong?'

Probably, but Edinburgh isn't making things easy. How hard can it be to drive to a major city and park a vehicle? Quite hard, actually. It shouldn't be, but it is.

Eventually, I give up on trying to find a satellite car park and simply drive towards Waverley Station, where we find what we're looking for. The parking charges are extortionate but we expected nothing less. We emerge on foot into an open-air car park littered with steel fencing and various building site paraphernalia. To our right is a small castle.

Is that.....? Can't be. I've been to Edinburgh before and I'm pretty certain that the castle is much bigger, and also down the other end of Princes Street. I ask a local if that's the castle, just to check.

'No. They call that thing 'Edinburgh's Disgrace'.'

'Why?'

'Sorry, I don't know.'

And she really didn't. The real 'Edinburgh's Disgrace' is an unfinished National Monument a little bit further out on Calton Hill, a proposed acropolis (or rather necropolis) dreamed up to house the famous dead of Scotland. Nineteenth century planners modelled the design on the Parthenon in Athens, and proposed the place as a kind of Scottish 'Valhalla' (no matter that Valhalla is actually a Norse concept). The project ran out of money, materialising only as a series of linked pillars, an eternal embarrassment to the city that couldn't find any more cash.

No, what we're actually looking at is the 'Governor's House', the last remaining section of the now demolished Calton Gaol. It looks very much like a miniature castle, and is very photogenic. It must be very nice inside as well because it's in the running as the official residence of Scotland's First minister.

We cut through the station, currently undergoing major renovation work in the public concourse, and head on up through to Princes Street. Words don't do justice to the view that opens up before us. Architecturally, Edinburgh is a feast for the eyes, and should be considered one of the most beautiful cities in modern Western civilisation. Standing in Princes Street alone, there are scores of impressive buildings in view, any one of which would mark the centrepiece of towns and smaller cities. Far from being a city of 'disgrace', it has an almost embarrassing number of richly designed, outstanding examples of superior architecture.

The Walter Scott Monument, stone blackened by almost two centuries of fumes, is a 200ft high gothic masterpiece pointing towards the sky. In the distance, at the far end of Princes Street, the real Edinburgh Castle squats on a craggy promontory, overlooking the city centre. Behind the greenery of Waverly Gardens stands the imposing, enormous building that's currently home to the Bank of Scotland. Even the shops lining the main thoroughfare are topped by interesting designs, perhaps the most spectacular of which is the Jenner's department store (owned by House of Fraser) dominating the corner of St David Street and Princes Street. Into this glorious mix are liberally sprinkled grandiose affairs such as the Royal Scottish Academy and the Scottish National Gallery. Everything I've mentioned is visible from where we're standing, a little way out of the station. It's a profusion of glorious design and I haven't even mentioned half of what's here.

We amble our way down towards the castle, soaking in the atmosphere. I'm not overly keen on big cities in general, particularly the way they all seem to homogenise over time, but Edinburgh really is something else. The thing I like best of all, even more than the sense of awe at being surrounded by the wondrous monolithic buildings, is that Edinburgh is also a place harbouring numerous hidden passages and winding side streets, some of which criss-cross each other at dizzying changes of elevation. It's like being inside an Escher painting. Walk along and you'll suddenly find yourself looking down on a different street eighty feet below. It's fantastic.

Steph tells me that the main reason she wanted to come to Edinburgh was to see the statue of Greyfriar's Bobby. For anyone familiar with the book (1912) or the film (1961), you'll already know that Bobby was a Skye Terrier with an almost supernatural love for a master he only spent two years with. John Gray, owner and inseparable companion for those 2 years, died of TB and was buried in Greyfriar's Kirk (which, if you have been paying attention, you'll know is the place where Robert the Bruce murdered John Comyn). For the next 14 years, little Bobby kept watch over the grave, awaiting his master's return. For dog lovers, it's one of the most heartbreaking stories ever told (second only to the folk-tale crystallised as the story of Gelert, the faithful hound who saves his master's baby from a wolf and is then killed by his master in the mistaken belief that Gelert had attacked the infant).

It gives me no pleasure in helping to debunk this myth, but it's unlikely to be true. There's no absolute proof that Bobby was even John Gray's dog, and may simply have been a nuisance dog evicted from the gardens of a nearby hospital. The 1912 book by Eleanor Atkinson replaced nightwatchman Gray with a shepherd called Auld Jock. Nobody really knows who the owner was for certain, or even if any part of the story is actually true. Despite this, Disney called their film version 'Greyfriars Bobby: The True Story of a Dog', something that could be looked at as a lie told to children to make the Disney Corporation lots of money. Ruthless bastards! James Brown, the curator of the graveyard, seemed to enjoy the company of the dog and found it brought in tips when visiting tourists paid him to hear the dog's story. It's entirely possible that Brown made the whole thing up as a way to encourage more tips, and the story became embedded as a cultural meme when it was published in a National newspaper, a news article that has ultimately brought about Steph's own desire to visit the site. And the city, in fact.

The statue we find, a small pillar designed as a drinking fountain (with 2 fountains, one for dogs and one for their masters), features a life-sized cast of a Skye Terrier perched on top. At one time, the dog faced in the direction of the graveyard, but now faces an entirely different direction that conveniently means that any tourist taking a photograph will always get a shot of the 'Greyfriars Bobby's Bar' in the background. This was presumably carried out under the instruction of a canny landlord, a simple act that has produced one of the most successful advertising campaigns ever seen.

It's interesting to note that this cute little doggy hasn't escaped the Scottish penchant for statue vandalism. Although Bobby never had his face hacked off (a la William Wallace / Mel Gibson), he did suffer the indignity of being painted yellow in 1979 and being hit by a car in 1984, although this may have been an accident and not an extreme form of deliberate vehicular carnage. The oddest form of defacement little Bobby has endured is undoubtedly having a mask of Donald Trump attached to his head, the result of a wave of National protest regarding the American tycoon's plans to build a new golf course near Aberdeen. That was in 2009. On the day of writing this, news is just in that the editor of Golf Monthly is urging players to boycott the new course after a recent BBC documentary alleged that Trump's organisation had bullied and intimidated local residents in an attempt to force them to sell their homes.

You can just imagine a residents meeting:

'This is a disgrace! This wiggy Yank prick wants to destroy areas of outstanding natural beauty, destroy long-term established wildlife habitats, and is trying to bully us into selling our homes.'

'Aye, he may take everything. But he'll never take…. Our FREEDOM!'

'Piss off Mel, who invited you? Come on people, what are we gonnae do about it?'

There's a long silence. Somebody puts their hand up at the back.

'Yes, Tam?'

'Well, I have this Donald Trump mask…..'

After a couple of drinks and a few photos, we head off in search of somewhere to eat a spot of lunch. Amazingly, for a city that uses Greyfriars Bobby as an enticement for tourism, the immediate area proves impossible to find an eaterie that will allow Clem to come inside and sit quietly at our feet. This is a particular shame in regard to the 'world famous' Frankenstein themed pub (complete with a hulking metal statue of the classic Karloff monster in the doorway), as we would have been perfectly willing to pay for their overpriced lunches just to be allowed to sit inside for a little while.

The only place we can find is at an outside table at the Kohl Bar. Outside dining tables in Scotland are not quite the same as the European set-ups they are trying to emulate. The most obvious difference is it's fucking freezing. We order our meals with a couple of drinks and no small amount of optimism. When they arrive, the wind literally blows the heat from the food before we can even get it into our mouths. We wolf down what we can and leave.

On the Royal Mile, we see a crowd of people surrounding a shirtless guy engaged in some sort of fire-eating act. He spends longer trying to encourage the audience to part with their money than he does eating fire. Steph wanders off, distracted by one of the tat stalls selling leather bracelets. She dithers for ages choosing one she likes. I can almost hear the escalating car park charges in the background. Still, this holiday hasn't been very enjoyable for her, so I try not to hurry her along, even after she finally makes a purchase and then proceeds to stop and gawp at every shop window display all the way back to the car park.

One of the shops entices us inside, but only after checking that we can take Clem in. That is the price of our potential custom. Steph buys a white hoody covered in 'Big Bang Theory' catchphrases, which is pretty cool. I see a zipless cardigan covered in skulls, which isn't my usual clobber of choice but it does look very stylish. I ask the staff if it's for men. It isn't, but they say a guy bought one for himself a few days ago. I don't think there's any danger of turning into Alex Reid if I buy myself a nice woman's cardy, so I try it on. I'm way too big for it, and I literally look like a man who has stuffed himself into a woman's cardigan. Steph bursts out laughing and the shop assistants look embarrassed for me. I'm gutted. Even more so when I see a woman's knitted jumper covered in yellow and black Batman logos. It's the coolest jumper I think I've ever seen.

'Do you have any of this stuff for men?' I ask.

'No, men don't usually buy things like this. T-shirts, loads, but this stuff… We used to stock it, ages ago, but it never sold.'

We walk to the van through the back streets, past the site for the Edinburgh

Ghost Tours and past walls covered in colourful flyers for upcoming bands. It's been a short visit, but Edinburgh has proven to be a thoroughly enjoyable place to spend a few hours. We make plans to come back again, soon.

We head to Berwick-upon-Tweed, driving some pleasant stretches close to the coast and passing by a couple of enormous industrial constructions, a concrete factory and a power station. Although English since 1482, Berwick has changed ownership many times, being central to the many border wars between England and Scotland. It has been taken with violence, laid siege to, and even ceded peaceably between the nations. To this day there are still people fighting to have the town brought back under Scottish control.

At one time, it was said to be '..so populous and of such commercial importance that it might rightly be called another Alexandria', although this was said a very long time ago – today, it's just another town that many English people have never even heard of.

It seems fitting, somehow, to round off the trip here. We're dropping the van back with Classic Camper Holidays in the morning, which is about an hour or so from here. This is our last night in Sally.

We find a campsite with a great view down to the harbour. Admittedly, there's a big row of council houses between us and the harbour, but the proles have to have somewhere to live, don't they?

I park up at Reception and get out. I'm immediately confronted by a small sign telling me to ring the doorbell and wait. A middle-aged woman emerges from a caravan at the side of the office. She looks me up and down. She obviously doesn't like the look of the riff-raff with the poor man's RV.

'Are we OK to stay here?' I ask, sensing her disapproval.

'Are you a member of the Caravan Club?'

'I think so. How much do you charge for a single night?'

'Are you a member of the Caravan Club?' she repeats, unwavering in her determination to get an answer.

'Yes, I am.'

'Where's your card?'

This feels like some sort of interrogation.

'I'll just go and fetch it,' I say, walking back to the van. She huffs and turns to unlock the office door before disappearing inside. I've a good mind to tell the snotty bitch where she can shove her campsite but after last night's fiasco I decide that I should just shut up and ignore her obvious hatred at the thought of allowing us to pitch up for the night. I grab the documents from the glovebox and head into the office.

She opens up the folder and shakes her head.

'There's no card. Is this a Caravan Club wallet?'

'I think so.'

'It says 'Camping and Caravanning Club'.'

Indeed it does.

'Ok. So, how much for a single night?' I ask.

'That's not us.'

'What's not us?'

'The 'Camping and Caravanning Club'. We're the 'Caravan Club'.'

'Is there any real difference?' I ask, ready to slit her throat and burn this part of Berwick into the sea.

I don't say that.

'Right,' I say. 'Can we stay here, or not?'

'It'll be £24.70 for one night.'

A bit steep, perhaps, but I smile and pay anyway. She produces a bit of paper with a site plan on it, and marks our pitch in blue marker. I realise that I have forgotten to mention Clem. Damn it, I've already paid. I wonder if we're going to get turfed out once I admit there's a dog.

'I have a little dog, is that OK?'

'Do not walk the dog anywhere inside the campsite. It must do its business outside.'

I thank her and leave. As we drive up to the pitch, I become aware of all the signage everywhere, all listing things that cannot be done:

No Walking of Dogs
No Driving Over 5mph
No Cycling
No Ball Games

What an utterly joyless, dismal way to run a campsite. There is a nice view from the pitch, but as well as the aforementioned council houses below, we're also surrounded by them above and behind as well. So, for all of the petty rules, and for all of Hyacinth Bouquet's disdain, it turns out that we're pretty much in the middle of a council estate!

I use the remaining daylight to give the van a good tidy. I take out all of our bits and bobs from the various cupboards and hidey-holes, and pack it all into the crates. Tomorrow morning, I'll just need to check the oil and we can shoot straight off to Hawick. Steph opens up a bottle of wine and I sit on a crate outside the van having a smoke and enjoying the view.

I make dinner. This involves opening a family pack of Doritos. Neither of us can be bothered to face anything more complicated.

Hawick - Home

We're up early and I reconfigure the van, unhook the electric and check the oil. We waste no time in getting off the site before we have a chance to break any of their rules.

Out of the town, we head into some beautiful and scenic countryside, crossing back and forth over the river Tweed. The roads are clear and we make good progress, enough to stop at Kelso and grab a bite to eat from an ASDA. Coffee and toast for Steph, coffee and a bacon roll for me – you wouldn't expect a supermarket café to deliver decent food but it does, and we happily sit in the van and munch it all down.

On the way out of town, I fill up the tank with petrol. Within the hour we reach Hawick, and even though the indicator is still showing full, I stop at another petrol station and fill her up to the brim with a second helping.

As we drive up the same narrow lanes we first encountered when we picked up Sally, it's clear that my driving is a lot more confident this time around. By now I'm fully used to the van and even comfortable with the left hand drive setup. And what a van it is – Sally has performed without fault, proving herself to be a solid and reliable vehicle. Despite the cold and the damp, which is pretty much all we could have expected out of a Scottish winter, we've enjoyed a unique trip and had a very thorough mooch around Scotland. Well, maybe I have – Steph did find herself stuck in the passenger seat looking after Clem on quite a few occasions.

Ian and Becca come out to greet us, and it's a very welcoming reception.

TERRA FIRMA TRAVELS

Little Fergus wastes no time in attracting Clem's attention and the two of them chase each other around the garden.

Ian looks knackered. It turns out that he had to go down to London yesterday to recover a van suffering from mechanical failure, a round trip that involved buying a trailer en route and then negotiating the streets of London attempting to track down the van. The danger of the business they are in is always going to be breakdowns, it's an unavoidable problem when dealing with older, classic vehicles. This time the problem was compounded by the vehicle being in France at the time of disaster, and a number of intercontinental phone calls resulted in the French mechanics asking for almost a thousand Euros to fix the problem.

Ian, a practical sort of bloke, knew that it would be far cheaper to get the vehicle back to the UK and get the issue fixed himself. All of this is something that always has a chance of happening, of course, but on top of all the bills they were looking at having to do a refund for the poor hirer. As a consequence of getting all of this sorted out, Ian didn't arrive back until the early hours.

Even so, he's in good spirits. I show him some of the trip photos and we chat for a little while about some of the places we went to. Then, without time for a break, he's off into Hawick to deal with something and we're left to finish up with Becca. They might be run ragged but they know that Winter will probably be quiet, so they're happy to deal with everything and put in the hours now and make hay whilst the sun's shining (figuratively speaking, of course).

I really like them, and I hope the business succeeds. If this book helps in attracting a few bookings for them, I'll be very happy. They offer a unique experience, one that has provided us with a way of thoroughly exploring Scotland on our own terms. We've dictated our own schedule and cut out the expense and bother of tracking down a different hotel every night. Although the weather has been pretty dire, we couldn't have asked for more, and Ian and Becca offered a level of service that we were extremely happy with. If a VW trip around Scandinavia ever turns into something that actually happens, I'll go straight to these guys for everything we'll need.

We stand chatting for so long that Ian returns before we set off home. We wave goodbye and then we're away, driving back down to Hawick in a car that feels strange, a toy car in comparison to the campervan. I can hardly see out of the rear windscreen for all of the crates and Steph no longer has acres of room to stretch her legs.

Clem snuggles into her lap and goes to sleep. Soon after, Steph is also dozing away. I'm left to drive home in relative silence. It's a long drive, but it gives me time to think back over the trip and marvel at just how much we managed to cram in. It starts to rain. Ah, the rain, our constant companion on our travels.

Poor Steph, this is another holiday she's coming back from without a tan.

Next time, I really must take her somewhere sunny.

Thank you for buying and reading this book. If you enjoyed it, please consider leaving a review on Amazon.
Thank you.

CLASSIC CAMPER HOLIDAYS

Classic Camper Holidays is a small, family-run VW Campervan rental company based in the beautiful Scottish Borders, offering a friendly, yet professional service. We have some of the best Campervans available for hire in Britain.

Our VW Camper vans range in age and style from 1972 to 2010 models, so we have something to suit all tastes. Whether it's something you've always wanted to do or you're simply curious as to what it's like, whether tootling along country lanes in a classic or holidaying in a modern camper is more up your street, we will provide you with an amazing campervanning experience that you'll never forget.

Our campers are all individual. Choose from either of our two beautifully restored 1970s original campers named Bluebell and Heidi, Daisy our 2010 Danbury T2, Sally our completely original left-hand-drive Westfalia, our 1990 T25 Autosleeper, Mr.T, or Oscar our new T5 Leisuredrive, who is the latest addition to the family! Each is unique and comes complete with extensive standard equipment, plus there are a host of extras available for hire to make your holiday even easier.

We were pleased that our innovative approach and focus on exemplary customer service were recognised in the 2010-2011 Scottish Borders Business Excellence Awards where we were shortlisted as a finalist in the Best New Business category.

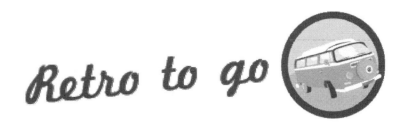

Meet our VW camper vans

We have three original pre-1979 camper vans, two of whom have been lovingly restored and refurbished to a very high standard, the third is an original left-hand-drive Westfalia with a few added extras, and we also have a two year old T2 Danbury, a 1990 T25, and a 2009 T5. Each of our vans are quite different and offer a variety of holiday experiences.

Oscar

Oscar is our new T5 Leisuredrive. Oscar provides luxury camping with the compact manouverability of a modern Camper Van! Available with or without wheelchair access. Oscar is available all year round.

Heidi

Heidi is full of retro charm! If you're looking to combine the fun original VW experience with a modern interior, then Heidi is the girl for you.

Daisy

Daisy is our brand new "classic" camper and offers an up-to-date, modern, slightly more roomy interior, with the exterior vintage styling of the 1970s.

Bluebell

Bluebell is referred to as a "tin top" as she has a non-raising roof. Originally converted in 1975, Bluebell has since been lovingly restored to her former glory with a modern cream leather interior. She's a pretty girl with her crome trim and dual colouring.

Sally

Sally is our left-hand drive T2 Westfalia. She's in beautiful condition with original fittings inside and out. Sally's vintage feel in such a beautiful van is highly sought after for the ultimate in retro experience.

Mr.T

Mr.T is our 1990 T25 Autosleeper. If your looking for a slightly more spacious camper then this is the dude for you. Mr.T still has that retro feel, but in a chunky cool 80's style which provides a robust and sturdy van. Mr.T is available all year round.

Kids Welcome

Our camper vans are ideal for holidaying with children, embodying the freedom of the open road and a sense of adventure. However, we also understand how important it is to keep children safe and comfortable. Our vans are fitted with modern 3 point seat belts that will accommodate most rear facing, forward facing and high-back booster seats. However, because of the low backed seats of the vans backless car seats and booster seats are not recommended. We cannot guarantee that all child seats will fit. Please contact us if you have any questions or need any help accessing a child seat.

Keeping You Safe

Safety standards have moved on enormously since the 1970s. At Classic Camper Holidays we apply industry best practice when it comes to preventative safety. From fitting modern laminate windscreens and conducting annual gas & electrical system safety tests, to performing weekly vehicle safety checks and providing fire extinguishers & fire blankets as standard in all of our campers.

Equipment & Extras

Our vans all come well equipped to ensure you have everything that you need for a great holiday. These are the items that you can expect to find as standard:

For the van...

Integral sink & cooker with spare gas cylander

Fridge (Sally has a built in coolbox fridge - we provide ice packs)

Integral petrol/gas-fired heater (Except Sally who has freestanding gas and electric heaters available)

12v leisure battery & cigarette lighter sockets

230v mains hook-up system & 3-pin plug sockets

Aux wire for connecting music players up to the vans sound system (except Oscar, but we're working on this)

Sun canopy and windbreak, Camping chairs with cup holder (for outside)

Torch & wind-up lantern, Leveling wheel chocks

Fire extinguisher, fire blanket, mini 1st aid kit & breakdown safety kit

Van info pack, Camping & Caravanning Club mambership pack

2013 Collins big road atlas, Scottish Borders street map, Scottish Campsites Map & various leaflets

For the kitchen...

Small kettle, Frying pan, saucepan and pot with lid

Grater, potato peeler, scissors, wooden spoons, colander

Melamine crockery and mugs, plastic tumblers & wine glasses, set of 4

Cutlery, set of 6 (except Bluebell, set of 4)

Tin/bottle opener & corkscrew, Chopping board and knife

Cafetiere/coffee filter, Oven mitt, tea towel & hand towel

Cleaning kit: Washing-up bowl, sponge, cloth, dish brush, washing-up liquid & surface spray

Hob toaster (in Heidi & Sally as they have no grill)

String & matches, Small supply of: salt, pepper, sugar, olive oil

The Campervan Cookbook

CLASSIC CAMPER HOLIDAYS
Retro to go

Hiring a VW campervan is a great adventure and renting with us is without doubt the best way to experience Scotland and northern England. Renting one of our campers will get you up close and personal with some of most stunning scenery and wildlife to be found in the UK. Scotland's access legislation means you can pull up in your van just about anywhere, just so long as you act responsibly and follow The Outdoor Access Code. That means there's no need to restrict yourself to staying at crowded camp sites. Find somewhere off the beaten track and wake up to a different, amazing view every morning.

You may or may not have heard that Classic vehicles can have a bit of a reputation for being unreliable! But the cause of this is that the vans are SO reliable that owners can become complacent with their maintenance, and this on top of the age of the vehicles is when problems can occur....

Therefore we endeavor to service and maintain each of our vehicles to the highest standard of working order so that you can enjoy your holiday with peace of mind.

We look forward to welcoming you on a holiday you'll always remember, for the right reasons.

Ian and Becca Anderson

+44 (0)8435 23 57 23
info@classic-camper-holidays.co.uk

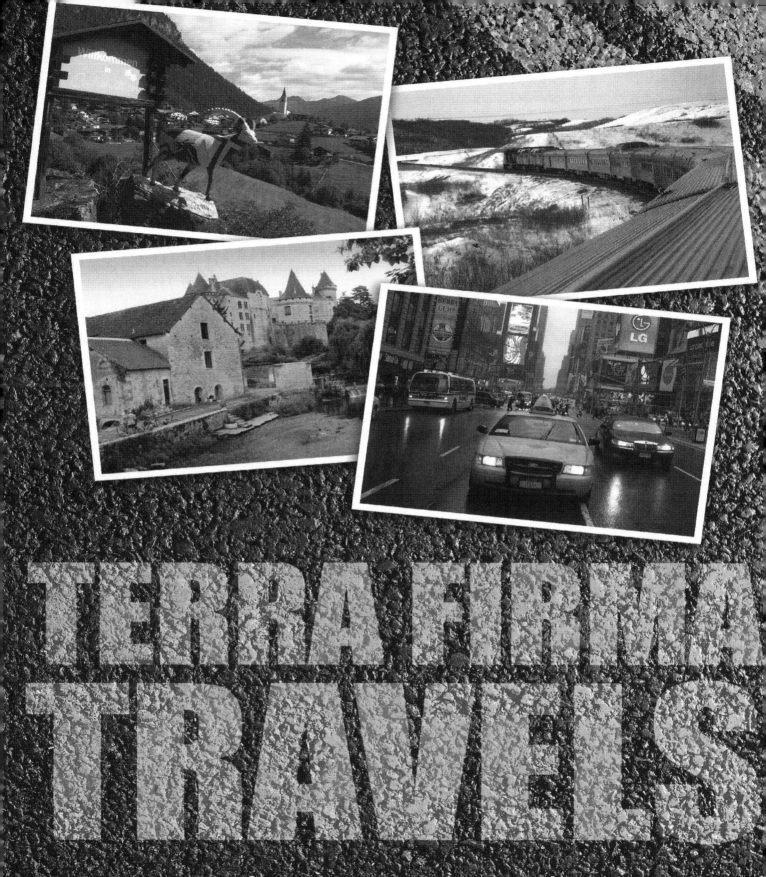

TERRA FIRMA TRAVELS

Aerophobic Adventures in Europe and North America

STEVE ROACH

TERRA FIRMA TRAVELS

All of Steve's travel books in a single volume compilation:-

Cycles, Tents and Two Young Gents

Step It Up!

Next Time, We're Flying Somewhere Sunny

Mountains, Lochs & Lonely Spots

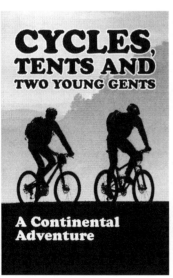
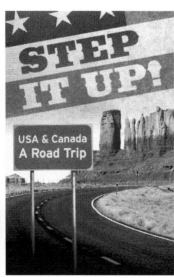

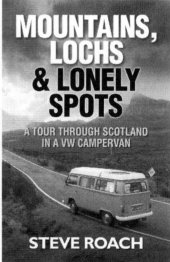

CYCLES, TENTS AND TWO YOUNG GENTS

A Continental Adventure

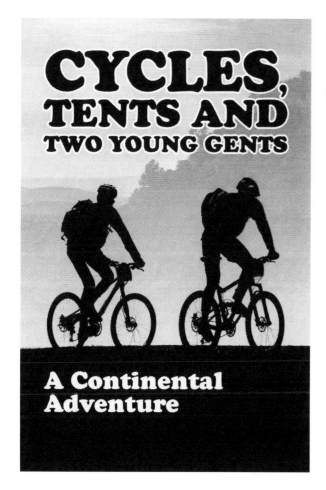

CYCLES, TENTS AND TWO YOUNG GENTS

Two friends embark upon an expedition through France, cycling from Cherbourg to Perpignan. Over the course of almost 1500 kilometres, they battle through the relentless heat and encounter vampire flies, angry restaurant proprietors and a host of European characters that have made France their playground for the Summer.

Along the way, they also contend with a rapidly diminishing cash supply, numerous dodgy camp sites and encounters with various French nutters. They are also forced to deal with perhaps the most difficult obstacle of all - each other!

A test of friendship and endurance, 'Cycles, Tents and Two Young Gents' puts you right alongside the hardy adventurers as they complete their grueling journey – the only difference is you won't finish the expedition with saddle sores and an empty bank account!

NEXT TIME, WE'RE FLYING SOMEWHERE SUNNY

Travels around Europe in a VW Campervan

'Packed with anecdotes and tales of adventure that will inspire any would-be traveller.'
Camper & Bus Magazine

Steve thought it would be a good idea to treat his girlfriend to a Grand Tour of Europe in a VW Campervan. They embark upon possibly the worst holiday ever. They discover that Campervans are really quite small, that the rain in Germany is endless and that Italy has no redeeming features whatsoever. A masterclass in misery.

NEXT TIME, WE'RE FLYING SOMEWHERE SUNNY

'Packed with anecdotes and tales of adventure that will inspire any would-be traveller.'
Camper & Bus Magazine

Steve thought it would be a good idea to treat his girlfriend to a Grand Tour of Europe in a VW Campervan. They embark upon possibly the worst holiday ever. They discover that Campervans are really quite small, that the rain in Germany is endless and that Italy has no redeeming features whatsoever. A masterclass in misery.

'Amazon Reviews:
Having read a few of Steve Roach's other books, and having always enjoyed his travelogues, I looked forward to this one. Opinionated, sometimes close to obnoxious but always interesting and very often funny - this one is no different. I'd always fancied the idea of a VW Campervan holiday - at least now, if I do, it I'll be armed with knowledge of things to bear in mind, like the turning distance of such vehicles and not to mention making sure your GPS is up to date for campsite locations.

I really enjoyed this. It perfectly describes the anticipation of a perfect break , and then the utter frustration when all does not go to plan , followed by the occasional moment of bliss when everything falls into place.

STEP IT UP!

USA & Canada A Road Trip

STEP IT UP!

Ever Wondered What It Would Be Like To Do A BIG Road Trip in the USA? Find out from the comfort of your armchair!

North America is a big place - huge, in fact - and the author and his girlfriend spent 3 months seeing as much of it as they could by car, train, bus and even snowmobiles. They covered about 12,000 miles in all, taking in 30 US States, Canada and even a bit of Mexico.

From the big cities (New York, San Francisco, Toronto, New Orleans) to the rural beauty of the American wilderness (Big Sur, Yosemite, Grand Canyon, Monument Valley) they tried to fit in as much as they could.

They went snowmobiling in the Canadian Rockies and saw an Ultimate Fighting Championship event in Las Vegas. They stayed in an ice hotel, went to Disneyland and Niagara Falls. They went to Florida Keys, New England and the Deep South, and were chased out of Georgia by a car full of murderous locals!

Join the author and his long-suffering girlfriend on the trip of a lifetime. A hundred joyful experiences punctuated with bouts of boring driving and nights in some seriously scary motels, this is a warts-and-all account of an enormous journey told with (sometimes) brutal honesty.

Amazon Reviews:
I've been thinking about going to the States for a while now and have bought one or two travel guides. They show a lot of pictures and list a lot of hotels, but they don't really tell you what a place is like to travel through. This book is all about the travel! From New York to New York by way of New England, Canada, Vancouver, San Francisco, Arizona, New Orleans and a hundred other places in between, I felt like I was right there with them.

ALSO AVAILABLE ON AMAZON:

PAPERBACKS

  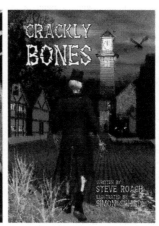 

KINDLE EBOOKS

DESK DIARIES

   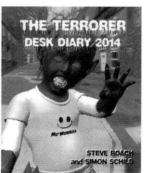

Printed in Great Britain
by Amazon